"Horses at night"

Frank Mechau
1934

Walking Denver

Stewart M. Green

Bryant's

bpatton4@du.edu

things to do:
Botannic Garden
Red Rocks

AVA Endorsed by the American Volkssport Association

Zoo
V.P. letter to see Mint.
Outlying parks for hiking.
Cherry Creek Shopping Mall.
Sheep skin rugs - on 16th

FALCON® HELENA, MONTANA

A FALCON GUIDE®

Falcon® Publishing is continually expanding its list of recreational guide-books. All books include detailed descriptions, accurate maps, and all the information necessary for enjoyable trips. You can order extra copies of this book and get information and prices for other Falcon guidebooks by writing Falcon, P.O. Box 1718, Helena, MT 59624 or calling toll-free 1-800-582-2665. Also, please ask for a free copy of our current catalog. Visit our web site at http:// www.falconguide.com

©1998 by Falcon Publishing, Inc., Helena, Montana.
Printed in Canada.

1 2 3 4 5 6 7 8 9 0 TP 03 02 01 00 99 98

Falcon and FalconGuide are registered trademarks of Falcon® Publishing, Inc.

Cover photo by Stewart M. Green.

All black-and-white photos by Stewart M. Green unless otherwise noted.

Cataloging-in-Publication Data is on record at the Library of Congress.

CAUTION

Outdoor recreational activities are by their very nature potentially hazardous. All participants in such activities must assume the responsibility for their own actions and safety. The information contained in this guidebook cannot replace sound judgment and good decision-making skills, which help reduce risk exposure, nor does the scope of this book allow for disclosure of all the potential hazards and risks involved in such activities.

Learn as much as possible about the outdoor recreational activities in which you participate, prepare for the unexpected, and be cautious. The reward will be a safer and more enjoyable experience.

 Text pages printed on recycled paper.

Contents

the walks

West Denver

South Denver

Lakewood

Golden

Boulder

Outta Town

Appendices

Acknowledgments

Denver is just up the road from my hometown of Colorado Springs. It's always been a special city to me, a place to go for arts and entertainment, concerts, sporting events, great restaurants, and, finally, great walking tours.

I owe a special thank you to my Denver walking companion, Martha Morris, for her help in selecting these excellent walks, taking notes along the trails and sidewalks, editing and commenting on the manuscript, and creating the book's maps.

Additional thanks go to Judith Galas and Cindy West, editors of the Walking America's Cities series at Falcon Publishing, for suggestions and comments. Thanks also go to former guidebook editor Randall Green and publisher Bill Schneider, who gave me the opportunity to contribute to Falcon's great book list. Thanks are due Greg Neitzke with the Denver Department of Parks and Recreation; Jeff Shoemaker with the Greenway Foundation; and staff members at the Denver Convention and Visitor Bureau, Roxborough State Park, Castlewood Canyon State Park, and the Golden Chamber of Commerce. I also offer thanks to Eric Green, who guided me toward some of Golden's history and points of interest, and to Ed Webster, who suggested the inclusion of Mapleton Hill in the Boulder walk.

Lastly, *gracias* to Nancy Spencer-Green, who walked the walk and put up with the talk, and to Ian and Brett Spencer-Green, two cool guys who supplied me with sunglasses and good tunes.

Foreword

For almost twenty years, Falcon has guided millions of people to America's wild outside, showing them where to paddle, hike, bike, birdwatch, fish, climb, and drive. With this walking series, we at Falcon ask you to try something just as adventurous. We invite you to experience this country from its sidewalks instead of its back roads, and to stroll through some of the United States' most interesting cities.

In their haste to get where they are going, travelers often bypass our country's cities. In the process, they miss historic and scenic treasures hidden among the bricks. Many people seek spectacular scenery and beautiful settings on top of mountains, along rivers, and in woods. Although nothing can replace the serenity and inspiration of America's natural wonders, our urban landscapes have their own kind of beauty.

The steel and glass of a city's "municipal mountains" reflect sunlight and make people feel small in the shadows. Birds sing in city parks and water burbles in fountains. Along the sidewalks visitors can still see abundant wild life—their fellow human beings.

We hope that Falcon's many guidebooks have encouraged you to explore and enjoy America's natural beauty, while working to preserve and protect it. Our cities also are meant to be explored and enjoyed; their irreplaceable treasures also need care and protection.

When travelers want to explore someplace that is inspiring and beautiful, we hope they will lace up their walking shoes and point their feet toward a city. There, along the walkways, they are sure to discover the excitement, history, beauty, and charm of urban America.

—*Judith Galas and Cindy West, Editors*

Map Legend

Walk Route		River or Stream		
Interstate Highways		Lake or Pond		
Streets and Roads		Boundary, State Park, or Institution		
Hiking/Walking Trail		Interstate		25
Start/Finish of Loop Walk	S/F	U.S. Highway		40
Parking Area	P	State and County Roads		36
Building		Railroad		+++++++
Church or Cathedral	✝	Map Orientation		N
Restrooms, Male and Female	👫	Scale of Distance	0 0.5 1 Miles	
Handicapped Access	♿	Overlook or Point of Interest		◘
Picnic Area	🪑	Gate		⊢
Playground				
Tennis Courts				

Overview Map

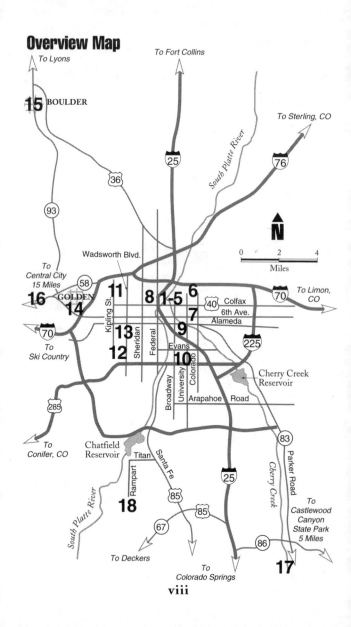

Preface: Come Walk Denver

Before trains, automobiles, and airplanes, a maze of trails spread across North America, linking cities, villages, and farms with the far-flung frontier. Pioneers and gold seekers marched west along the Oregon, California, and Santa Fe trails. Colorado's first miners and townspeople trekked across the Great Plains on the Smoky Hill Trail or followed the Trappers Trail north and south along the Front Range.

Americans are again discovering the joys of foot travel, finding simple pleasures and physical fitness along the path. The National Trail System, established by Congress in 1968, now embraces eight National Scenic Trails, nine National Historic Trails, and more than eight hundred National Recreation Trails. Many are found in urban areas, some of them linking cities with the surrounding countryside.

Walking Denver is a superb sampler of Denver's urban walks, as well as a selection of unique nature hikes. Known as the "Mile High City," Denver and its surrounding suburbs offer hundreds of miles of urban trails. The routes thread through parks and open space, alongside many more miles of sidewalks lining city streets. Visitors and residents alike can discover numerous hikes and rambles to suit their fancy and level of fitness.

Explore old Auraria, where Denver began. Take in the bustling warehouse district of Lower Downtown, or the stately government district around Civic Center Park. Saunter on the University of Denver campus. Discover lakes and trees in parklands such as City Park, Washington Park, and Sloan Lake Park. Farther afield, delight in Boulder's eccentric Pearl Street Mall, or in the historic buildings and mines at Central City. Experience nature amid the soaring sandstone formations at Roxborough State Park, or at the abrupt prairie canyon at Castlewood Canyon State Park.

The walks detailed in this book are easy to find and fol-low. Their lengths and levels of difficulty vary, but most are easily accomplished in a few hours. Many routes are barrier-free, accessible to people in wheelchairs. An interpretative text describes each walk, giving detailed directions and point-ing out important landmarks, historic sites and buildings, and points of interest. The variety of trails and sidewalks explored here is matched only by Denver's eclectic diversity.

Enough talking. It's time to hit the sidewalk and start walking!

Introduction

Walking a city's boulevards and avenues can take you into its heart and give you a feel for its pulse and personality. Looking up from the sidewalk, you can appreciate a city's architecture. Peeking in from the sidewalk, you can find the quaint shops, local museums, and great eateries that give a city its charm and personality. From a city's nature paths, you can smell the flowers, glimpse the wildlife, gaze at a lake, or hear a creek gurgle, and only from the sidewalk can you get close enough to read the historical plaques and watch the people.

When you walk a city, you get it all—adventure, scenery, local color, good exercise, and fun.

How to use this guide

We have designed this book so that you can easily find the walks that match your interests, time, and energy level. Walks at a Glance is the first place you should look when deciding on a walk. This table will give you the basic information—a walk's distance, estimated walking time, and difficulty. The pictures or icons in the table also tell you specific things about the walk:

If you like to take pictures, you will get some scenic shots or vistas on this walk. Every walk has something of interest, but this icon tells you that the route has great views of the city or the surrounding area. Be sure to bring your camera.

Somewhere along the route you will have the chance to get food or a beverage. You will have to glance through the walk description to determine where and what kind of food and beverages are available. Walks that do not have the food icon probably are along nature trails or in non-commercial areas of the city.

1

During your walk you will have the chance to shop. More detailed descriptions of the types of stores you will find can be found in the actual walk description.

This walk has something kids will enjoy seeing or doing—a park, zoo, museum, or play equipment. In most cases the walks that carry this icon are shorter and follow an easy, fairly level path. You know your young walking companions best. If your children are patient walkers who do not tire easily, then feel free to choose walks that are longer and harder. In fact, depending on a child's age and energy, most children can do any of the walks in this book. The icon only notes those walks we think they will especially enjoy.

Your path will take you primarily through urban areas. Buildings, small city parks, and paved paths are what you will see and pass.

You will pass through a large park or walk in a natural setting where you can see and enjoy nature.

The wheelchair icon means that the path is fully accessible and that it would also be an easy walk for anyone in a wheelchair or pushing a stroller. We have made every attempt to follow a high standard for accessibility. The icon means there are curb cuts or ramps along the entire route, plus a wheelchair-accessible bathroom somewhere along the course. The path is mostly or entirely paved, and ramps and non-paved surfaces are clearly described. If you use a wheelchair and have the ability to negotiate curbs and dirt paths or to wheel for longer distances and on uneven surfaces, you may want to skim the directions for the walks that do not carry this symbol. You may find other walks you will enjoy. If in doubt, read the full text of the walk or call the contact source for guidance.

A note to joggers: Joggers also can enjoy many of the walks in this book. If you prefer to jog, first look for those walks with a rating of 1 or 2. These walks most likely are flat and have a paved or smooth surface. If you want something more challenging, read the walk descriptions to see if the harder routes may also appeal to you.

At the start of each walk chapter, you will find specific information describing the route and what you can expect on your walk.

General location: Here you will get the walk's general location in the city or within a specific area.

Special attractions: Look here to find the specific things you will pass. If this walk has museums, historic homes, restaurants, or wildlife, it will be noted here.

Difficulty: We have designed or selected walking routes that an ordinary person in reasonable health can complete. The walks are rated from one to five, one being the easiest. But the ease or difficulty does not relate to a person's level of physical fitness. A walk with a rating of 5 can be completed by an average walker, but that walker may feel tired when he or she has completed the walk and may feel some muscle soreness.

How easy or hard something can be depends on each person. But here are some general guidelines of what the number rating indicates:

A walk rated as Easy or 1 is flat, with little or no hills. Most likely you will be walking on a maintained surface made of concrete, asphalt, wood, or packed dirt. The path will be easy to follow, and you will be only a block or so from a phone, other people, or businesses. If the walk is less than a mile, you may be able to walk comfortably in street shoes.

A walk rated as Moderate or 3 includes some hills, and a few may be steep. The path may include stretches of sand, dirt, gravel, or small crushed rock. The path is easy to follow, but you may not always have street or sidewalk signs, so you may have to check your map or directions. You may be as much as 0.5 miles from the nearest business or people. You should wear walking shoes.

A walk rated as Difficult or 5 probably has an unpaved path that includes rocks and patches of vegetation. The trail may have steep ups and downs, and you may have to pause now and then to interpret the walk directions against the natural setting. You will have to carry water, and you may be alone for long stretches during the walk. Walking shoes are a must, and hiking boots may be helpful.

Walks rated 2 or 4 fall somewhere in between. If you are in doubt, read the walking text carefully or call the listed contact for more information.

Distance and estimated time: This gives the total distance of the walk. The time allotted for each walk is based on walking time only, which is calculated at about 30 minutes per mile, a slow pace. Most people have no trouble walking 1 mile in 30 minutes, and people with some walking experience often walk a 20-minute mile. If the walk includes museums, shops, or restaurants, add sightseeing time to the estimate.

Services: Here you will find out if such things as restrooms, parking, refreshments, or information centers are available and where you are likely to find them.

Restrictions: The most commonly noted restriction is for pets, which almost always have to be leashed in a city. Most cities also have strict "pooper-scooper" laws, and they enforce them. But restrictions may also include the hours or days a museum or business is open, age requirements, or whether you

4

can ride a bike on the path. If there is something you cannot do on this walk, it will be noted here.

For more information: Each walk includes at least one contact source for you to call for more information. If an agency or business is named as a contact, you will find its phone number and address in Appendix B. This appendix also includes contact information for any business or agency mentioned anywhere in the book.

Getting started: Here you will find specific directions to the starting point. The majority of our walks are closed-loop walks, which means they begin and end at the same point. So, you do not have to worry about finding your car or your way back to the bus stop when your walk is over.

In those cities with excellent transportation, it may be easy, and sometimes even more interesting, to end a few walks away from the start point. When this happens, you will get clear directions on how to take public transportation back to your starting point.

If a walk is not a closed-loop walk, this section will tell you where the walk ends. But you will find the exact directions back to your starting point at the end of the walk's directions.

Some downtown walks can be started at any one of several hotels the walk passes. The directions will be for the main starting point, but we will tell you if it is possible to pick the walk up at other locations. If you are staying at a downtown hotel, it is likely that a walk passes in front of or near your hotel's entrance.

Public transportation: Many cities have excellent transportation systems; others have limited services. If it is possible to take a bus or commuter train to the walk's start point, you will find the bus or train noted here. You may also find some information about where the bus or train stops and how often and when it runs.

Overview: Every part of a city has a story. Here is where you will find the story or stories about the people, neighborhoods, and history connected to your walk.

The walk

When you reach this point, you are ready to start walking. In this section you will find not only specific and detailed directions, but you will also learn more about the things you are passing. Those who want only the directions and none of the extras, can find the straightforward directions by looking for the ➤.

What to wear

The best advice is to wear something comfortable. Leave behind anything that binds, pinches, rides up, falls down, slips off the shoulder, or comes undone. Otherwise, let common sense, the weather, and your own body tell you what to wear.

Your feet take the hardest pounding when you walk, so wear good shoes. Sandals, shoes with noticeable heels, or any shoe you rarely wear are not good choices. Some running shoes make superb walking shoes. Choose running shoes with wide heels, little or no narrowing under the arch, noticeable tread designs, and firm insoles.

If you will be walking in the sun, in the heat of the day, in the wind, or along a route with little or no shade, be sure to take along a hat or scarf. Gloves are a must to keep your hands warm and from chapping in the winter, and sunscreen is important year-round.

What to take

Be sure to take water. Strap a bottle to your fanny pack or tuck a small one in a pocket. If you are walking several miles with a dog, remember to take a small bowl so your pet can have a drink.

Carry some water even if you will be walking where refreshments are available. Several small sips taken throughout a walk are more effective than one large drink at the walk's end. Also avoid drinks with caffeine or alcohol, because they deplete rather than replenish your body's fluids.

A fanny pack also comes in handy. It can hold your water, as well as your keys, money, and sunglasses, and leaves your hands free to read your directions. If you will be gone for several hours and will walk where there are few or no services, a light backpack can carry beverages and snacks.

Safety and street savvy

Mention a big city and many people immediately think of safety. Some questions are frequently asked: Is it safe to walk during the day? What about at night? What areas should I avoid?

Safety should be a common sense concern whether you are walking in a small town or a big city, but safety does not have to be your overriding concern. America's cities are enjoyable places, and if you follow some basic tips, you will find that these cities are also safe places.

Any safety mishap in a large city is likely to come from petty theft and vandalism. So, the biggest tip is simple: Do not tempt thieves. Purses dangling on shoulder straps or slung over your arm, wallets peeking out of pockets, arms burdened with packages, valuables on the car seat—all of these things attract the pickpocket, purse snatcher, or thief because you look like someone who could be easily relieved of your possessions.

Do not carry a purse. Put your money in a money belt or tuck your wallet into a deep side pocket of your pants or skirt or in a fanny pack that rides over your hip bone or

Trip Planner

the walks

Walk name	Difficulty	Distance (miles)	Time	♿	🏛	❀	🔊	📖	🍴	📷
Downtown										
1. Civic Center	easy/1	1	1.5 hrs	✓	✓		✓			✓
2. 16th Street Mall	easy/1	1.3–2.6	1.5 hrs	✓	✓			✓	✓✓	
3. Historic Lower Downtown	easy/1	1.5	1 hr	✓	✓			✓	✓✓	
4. Old Auraria	easy/1	2	1 hr	✓	✓					
5. South Platte River Greenway	easy/1	2	1.5 hrs	✓		✓	✓		✓	✓✓
6. The Grand Tour	moderate/2	10	5 hrs	✓	✓	✓	✓	✓	✓	✓✓
East Denver										
7. City Park	easy/1	1.5	1.5 hrs			✓	✓	✓	✓✓	✓✓
8. Cheesman Park–7th Avenue	easy/1	3	2 hrs	✓	✓	✓	✓	✓	✓✓	✓✓
West Denver										
9. Sloan Lake Park	easy/1	2.3	1.5 hrs	✓		✓	✓	✓	✓	✓
South Denver										
10. Washington Park	easy/1	2	1.5 hrs	✓		✓	✓		✓	
11. University of Denver	easy/1	1.5	1 hr	✓		✓			✓	

	Rating	Distance	Time	Good for kids	Shopping	Food	Bring camera
Lakewood							
12. Crown Hill Park	easy/1	1.9	1 hr	✓		✓	✓✓✓
13. Bear Creek Greenbelt	easy/2	2	1 hr			✓	✓✓
14. Belmar Park	easy/2	1.5	1 hr	✓		✓	✓
Golden							
15. Historic Golden	moderate/3	2	1.5 hrs		✓	✓	✓
Boulder							
16. Pearl Street Mall–Mapleton Hill	easy/2	1.1	1 hr	✓	✓	✓	✓
Out of town							
17. Central City	moderate/3	0.8	1 hr	✓	✓		
18. Castlewood Canyon State Park	difficult/5	2.04	1-3 hrs			✓✓	✓✓✓
	easy/1	.7					
19. Roxborough State Park	difficult/4	2.2	2 hrs			✓✓	✓✓✓✓

9

the icons

Wheelchair access	City Setting	Nature Setting	Good for kids	Shopping	Food	Bring camera

stomach. Lock your valuables in the trunk of your car before you park and leave for your walk. Protect your camera by wearing the strap across your chest, not just over your shoulder. Better yet, put your camera in a backpack.

You also will feel safer if you remember the following:
- Be aware of your surroundings and the people near you.
- Avoid parks or other isolated places at night.
- Walk with others.
- Walk in well-lit and well-traveled areas.
- Stop and ask directions if you get lost.

The walks in this book were selected by people who had safety in mind. No walk will take you through a bad neighborhood or into an area of the city that is known to be dangerous. So relax and enjoy your walk.

Share the fun

We have tried to walk you to and through the best this city has to offer. But you surely will discover other wonderful things—a fabulous bakery, a park tucked inside a neighborhood, a historic tidbit, or interesting museum. Be sure to write us to share your discovery. We would love to hear from you.

Meet Denver

Fast facts
General
    County: Denver
    Time zone: Mountain
    Area code: 303
Size
    Colorado's largest city
    481,700 people
    2,047,207 people in metro area
    4,503 square miles in metro area
    Number of communities: 40
Elevation
    5,280 feet above sea level at State Capitol
Climate
    Average yearly precipitation: 15.4 inches
    Average yearly snowfall: 60 inches
    Average yearly rainfall: 11 inches
    Average humidity: 67 percent A.M., 40 percent P.M.
    Average yearly days of sunshine: 245
    Average summer temperatures: 56-85 degrees F
    Average winter temperatures: 18-45 degrees F

Getting there
Major highways
    Interstates: I-25, I-70, and I-76
    U.S. highways: 6, 36, 40, 85, 285, and 287 State
    highways: 2, 30, 72, 74, 83, 88, 93, 121, 170, and 470
Airport service
    Air Canada, Continental Airlines, Delta Air Lines,
    Frontier Airlines, TransWorld Airlines,
    USAir, United Airlines

Bus service

Regional Transportation District (RTD) throughout city and suburbs.

Train service

Amtrak, Light Rail (5.3-mile route in South Denver)

Recreation

Golf courses: More than 50 (7 public)

Urban trails: More than 150 miles

Parks: Denver Parks and Recreation, Denver Mountain Parks, Jefferson County Open Space. Nearby Colorado State Parks include: Barr Lake, Castlewood Canyon, Eldorado Canyon, Golden Gate Canyon, and Roxborough, along with Chatfield and Cherry Creek State Recreation Areas.

Fishing: Many lakes, ponds, creeks, and rivers

Nearby ski areas: Arapahoe Basin, Breckenridge, Copper Mountain, Loveland, Keystone, Vail, and Winter Park

Nearby rock climbing areas: Boulder Canyon, Castlewood Canyon, Clear Creek Canyon, Eldorado Canyon, Flatirons, Golden Cliffs, Rocky Mountain National Park, and South Platte River

Major industries

Tourism, computers, electronics, government, and manufacturing

Media

Newspapers:

Boulder Daily Camera, Denver Business Journal, Denver Post, Rocky Mountain News, Westword

Radio stations:

More than 40, including:

KOA 850 AM—News, weather, talk, sports

KTLK 760 AM—News, talk, sports

KGNU 88.5 FM—National Public Radio, alternative and folk music

KCFR 90.1 FM—National Public Radio, classical music
KVOD 99.5 FM—Classical music
KYGO 950 AM and 98.5 FM—Country
KBCO 97.3 FM—Alternative rock

Television stations

KMGH (ABC)—Channel 7
KUSA (CBS)—Channel 9
KCNC (NBC)—Channel 4
KRMA (PBS)—Channel 6
KWGN (Independent)—Channel 2

Special annual events

Call the Denver Metro Convention and Visitors Bureau at 303-892-1112 for dates, places, and a complete list of all area events.

• January: National Western Stock Show, Annual Colorado Cowboy Poetry Gathering (Arvada)
• March: St. Patrick's Day Parade, Denver March Pow-wow
• May: Cinco de Mayo Celebration/Cultural Festival, Historic Denver Week, Bolder Boulder Race (Boulder)
• June: Juneteenth Celebration
• June and July: Colorado Renaissance Festival (Larkspur)
• July: Cherry Creek Arts Festival, Denver Black Arts Festival, Buffalo Bill Days (Golden), Gold Rush Days (Idaho Springs)
• August: Adams County Fair and Rodeo (Brighton), Douglas County Fair (Castle Rock)
• September: Annual Gem and Mineral Show, Gateway to the Rockies Festival (Aurora)
• October: Rocky Mountain Book Festival, Colorado Performing Arts Festival, Great American Beer Festival, Denver International Film Festival

• November and December: World's Largest Christmas Lighting Display

• December: Olde Golden Christmas (Golden), Parade of Lights

Spectator sports

Baseball: Colorado Rockies (NL)

Basketball: Denver Nuggets (NBA), Colorado Xplosion

Football: Denver Broncos (NFL), CU Buffaloes

Hockey: Colorado Avalanche (NHL), DU Pioneers

Soccer: Colorado Rapids

Dining

More than two thousand restaurants, including Chinese, Continental, French, Indian, Italian, Japanese, Mexican, and Vietnamese cuisines. "Colorado cuisine" includes buffalo, wild game, and rattlesnake. Denver has been nicknamed "the Napa Valley of Beer," with more beer brewed annually than any other city in the United States.

In the know

Weather

Contrary to what's spread around the rest of the country on nightly newscasts, the weather in Denver is surprisingly mild. Nestled in the broad South Platte River valley, the city is protected from many severe storms by the lofty Rocky Mountains. When Chicago or Los Angeles newscasters report that 20 inches of snow have fallen in Colorado in the past twenty-four hours, they are usually referring to mountain snowpack. Often, while snow-laden clouds obscure the Continental Divide and dump fresh powder on the ski slopes, Denver is basking in a 50-degree January day.

The mountains receive most of the moisture from Pacific storms that track across Colorado, leaving scant snowfall for the arid city. Denver's average precipitation is 15.4 inches, with an average snowfall of 60 inches and an average rainfall of 11 inches. The high altitude and low humidity make for pleasant summers and mild winters. Most snowfall melts within a week, although a prolonged spell of arctic air occurs at least once each winter. January's average daytime high is 41 degrees F. The sun shines a lot here, too; on average, there are 115 clear days and 130 partly cloudy days. July is the hottest month, with an average high of 88 degrees F. A handful of summer days reach the 100-degree mark each summer, but the low humidity makes them bearable.

Denver's weather is changeable. It can be summed up with the old folk saying, "If you don't like the weather, wait fifteen minutes!" Chinook winds, warming as they sweep off the mountains, are the famed "snow-eaters." They've been known to raise temperatures as much as 36 degrees in two hours, and blow as hard as 140 miles per hour. Localized thunderstorms often occur on summer afternoons, bringing high winds, heavy rain, damaging hail, and lightning. Keep an eye on the weather when you're out walking, particularly in the foothills, and be prepared for quick weather changes. Carry warm clothes, including gloves and a warm cap in winter. In summer, pack a raincoat, sun hat, and drinking water.

Transportation

By car: Denver is fairly easy to get around in by car. Numerous highways and boulevards allow easy access to most quarters of town. When the town was initially laid out in 1859, the streets were made parallel to Cherry Creek. As Denver grew into a larger city, these diagonal streets were surrounded by an east-west grid of streets that reached into the suburbs. The diagonal streets downtown are at odds with the rest of the city streets, making directions sometimes confusing to newcomers. Still, it's almost impossible to get lost in Denver, especially on a clear day. To orient yourself, just remember that the mountains are always to the west.

Denver's two main streets are Broadway, running north to south, and Colfax Avenue, running east to west. Routes labeled "streets" run north-south, although some may be "boulevards" or "drives." "Avenues" are roads that run east-west; Broadway is the east-west dividing line. Major north-south streets are Colorado, University, Santa Fe, Federal, and Sheridan boulevards. Sheridan divides Denver from the western suburbs. Major east-west avenues are Sixth, Alameda, Hampden, Bellview, and Arapahoe.

Major highways are north-south Interstate 25 (which connects Denver with Colorado Springs and Cheyenne, Wyoming), Interstate 70 (which runs west into the mountains and east to Kansas), and Interstate 76 (which heads northeast to Nebraska and I-80). Interstate 225 makes a loop from I-25 to I-70 across Denver's eastern suburbs. Major U.S. highways are US 6, up Clear Creek Canyon from Golden to Central City; US 285 from Denver to Fairplay and Buena Vista; and US 36 from Denver to Boulder and on to Estes Park. Colorado Highway 470 is a limited-access superhighway that forms a beltway around the south and west sides of Denver.

Parking is readily available in Denver, with many private and public parking lots. Metered parking is found on most city streets.

By bus: The Regional Transportation District (RTD) offers local, express, and regional bus service to Denver and the surrounding communities. Obtain schedules and route information from RTD by calling 303-299-6000, or stopping by the Market Street Station at Market and 16th streets downtown. Free shuttle buses regularly run up and down the 16th Street Mall. RTD also runs a light rail service on a 5.3-mile route from 30th Avenue to downtown.

By air: Denver International Airport (DIA) is 24 miles northeast of downtown Denver. The airport is accessed via Peña Boulevard at Exit 284 on I-70. This exit is easily reached from I-225 and I-25. The airport is served by RTD buses, taxis, shuttle limos, and rental cars.

With three concourses and a main terminal, DIA is unique. The terminal roof is composed of thirty-four Teflon-coated fiberglass tents that symbolize the Rocky Mountains. The airport spreads across 53 square miles, larger than both the Dallas–Fort Worth airport and Chicago's O'Hare International Airport. It is served by many major airlines.

By train: Denver's historic Union Station in Lower Downtown is still served by Amtrak's scenic California Zephyr route. In winter, Ski Train carries passengers to Winter Park.

Safety

As in any large city, walkers in Denver need to be safety-conscious to avoid any problems. Denver is safe, especially in its well-traveled and busy areas. Follow basic precautions and you shouldn't have to worry about your personal safety as you walk.

Whenever you travel or work in an unfamiliar city, stay alert. Be aware of your surroundings and the people around you. Wear a money belt instead of carrying a wallet, particularly if you plan to be in crowded spaces such as sporting events or festivals. Walk during daylight hours, especially in parts of the city with which you are unfamiliar. Take solace in the fact that tourists are rarely the victims of violent crimes.

If you park your car in remote parking areas or along roadways, make sure it is locked and all valuables and packages are hidden. Auto break-ins do occur at Denver-area trailheads and along city streets, especially at night. If you plan to stay several days, it's often safer to spend the extra money to park in a secured garage.

Carry drinking water in summer to protect yourself from dehydration. Water is not always available on the walks. Drinking fountains in parks may be out of service, or stores may be closed. Don't drink from any open streams or lakes. Most of them now harbor giardia, intestinal parasites that cause diarrhea, bloating, and other complications. Water from sprinklers in city parks is also non-potable.

At Denver's elevation, it's a good idea to wear a hat to protect your head from the sun's harmful rays. Use sunscreen, even on cloudy days. In winter, wear a hat, gloves, and a warm jacket since the weather can be windy and cold. You also may need boots for walking in snow.

The Story of Denver

Denver, in the afternoon shadow of the Rocky Mountains, owes its founding to the discovery of gold flakes near the confluence of the South Platte River and Cherry Creek. The story begins with William Greeneberry Russell, a dapper man from Georgia with a waxed mustache and a braided red beard, who led a group of prospectors on a search for paydirt in Pikes Peak country in 1858. Russell's party found a few hundred dollars worth of placer gold along the South Platte before moving west to prospect the Front Range canyons. Word of the group's meager gold discoveries made its way eastward, however, and the news was embellished and exaggerated as it traveled. When the Georgians returned to their South Platte diggings, they found the place swarming with fellow miners.

In October, Russell and his men founded a town on the south bank of Cherry Creek and dubbed it Auraria after their Georgia hometown, a name ironically derived from the Latin word for gold. With winter's onset, they headed east for supplies, passing General William Larimer at Bent's Fort on their way. Larimer headed north to Auraria, crossed the creek, and jumped the claim of another townsite. He dubbed his new settlement Denver to curry favor with the territorial governor, James Denver, unaware that Denver had resigned the post. The residents of Auraria and Denver quickly became rivals. Eventually, the arrival of a stagecoach line to Denver doomed Auraria, and the two towns peacefully consolidated on April 6, 1860, as Denver City.

The city's fortunes and population alternately rose and plummeted with the nearby mountain gold mining camps. Denver, with a population of 5,000, was filled with poor prospectors, industrious merchants, civic-minded townspeople, and slick land promoters, as well as desperadoes, gamblers, "soiled doves," and other assorted riffraff. Famous newspaperman Horace Greeley stopped by Denver en route to the Central City diggings and noted that there were "more brawls, more pistol shots with criminal intent in this log city of 150 dwellings . . . than in any community of equal numbers on earth." "Uncle Dick" Wooten, a trader of Santa Fe Trail fame, said "stealing was the only occupation of a considerable portion of the population." Law-abiding citizens took matters into their own hands to clean up the town, doling out liberal doses of frontier justice that usually left offenders dangling by the neck from a handy lamppost or cottonwood tree along Cherry Creek.

Denver grew and matured, becoming first the capital of Colorado Territory in 1867 and then the state capital when Colorado was admitted to the Union in 1876. The city's real growth and prosperity came with the arrival of the railroad in 1870. The rails linked Denver and its lucrative mining industry with the rest of the nation, transforming the raucous mining camp into a business and transportation hub. Though the gold rush abated, silver strikes in the late 1870s at Leadville, Aspen, and Georgetown renewed the boom, bringing more good times to the "Queen City of the Plains." Between 1880 and 1890, Denver's population grew almost 300 percent, from 36,629 to 106,713. Buildings, warehouses, foundries, manufacturing plants, and two smelters were erected. The mountain wealth also built elegant theaters, ornate mansions, and the finest restaurants and shops between St. Louis and San Francisco. However, the collapse of the world silver market in 1893 dropped Denver into a severe depression.

By 1900, Denver's economy had recovered and begun to improve again. Mayor Robert W. Speer addressed the city's quality of life by instituting "City Beautiful" ordinances, which spurred creation of what is now the nation's largest park system. He also spearheaded the landscaping of Cherry Creek, the creation of the Speer Boulevard parkway, the paving of city streets, the planting of thousands of trees, and the construction of new municipal buildings, including the Denver Civic Center.

During the Great Depression of the 1930s, Denver became known as "Cow Town," a moniker that took decades for its chamber of commerce to live down. Circa 1930, the Monfort family came up with the idea of raising and fattening cattle on hay and corn in feedlots instead of letting them roam the sparse Colorado range. Feedlots became Denver's feedbag, with railroad lines hauling cattle to the city's huge stockyards before shipping them off to the nation's meat markets.

After World War II, Denver again boomed as the "Mile-High City." Military and government installations, including the Denver Federal Center, Lowry Air Force Base, the Rocky Mountain Arsenal, and Fitzsimmons Army Medical Center, along with the U.S. Air Force Academy and Fort Carson in nearby Colorado Springs, were major contributors to the area's economy. In the 1970s and early 1980s, Denver became a national center for oil, oil shale, natural gas, coal, and solar energy development. New skyscrapers soared over downtown, dwarfing old Denver's stone and brick buildings. But when the energy business took a big tumble in the mid-1980s, Denver's glass-and-steel downtown emptied as companies moved or went bankrupt. The city's diversity kept it afloat—it had more federal workers than any other U.S. city except Washington, D.C., the military paycheck, and assorted high-tech and manufacturing companies to keep it going until prosperity, population, and steady growth returned in the 1990s.

Today, Denver is the economic and transportation hub of the western Rocky Mountains. Its historic downtown areas have been revitalized into bustling arts and business centers. The South Platte River corridor has shed its urban blight and has become instead a magnet for Denverites with museums, green space, and recreational opportunities. Denver residents are sports and recreation crazy. Denver is one of the only cities that owns teams in all four major league sports—the NFL Denver Broncos, the NHL Stanley Cup champion Colorado Avalanche, the NBA Denver Nuggets, and the National League baseball Colorado Rockies. Its close proximity to world-class ski areas, rock climbing cliffs, hiking and running trails, and bicycle paths make it an attractive city for outdoor enthusiasts. The surrounding towns and suburbs, including Boulder, Golden, and Central City, also share in Denver's dreams. In the end, former mayor Frederico Peña's slogan "Imagine a Great City" has finally come true.

Walk 1

Civic Center Walk

General location: A loop walk around Civic Center Park with numerous points of interest, including the State Capitol.

Special attractions: Denver Metro Convention and Visitors Bureau, U.S. Mint, City and County Building, Denver Art Museum, Byers-Evans Historic House, Denver Public Library, Colorado History Museum, Colorado Supreme Court Building, Colorado State Capitol, war memorials, western statues.

Difficulty rating: Easy. The walk is barrier-free and suitable for small children.

Distance: 1 mile.

Estimated time: 1 hour to 1 day, depending on how much time you spend exploring the various museums.

Services: All services can be found within a few blocks of

Civic Center Walk

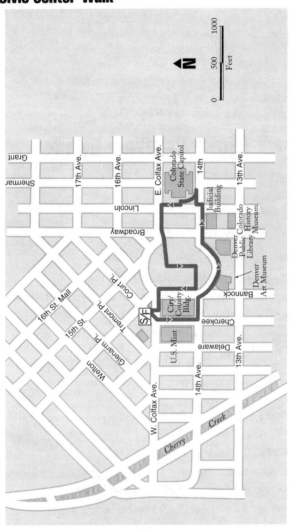

the walk, including parking garages, restrooms in public buildings, restaurants, and the Convention and Visitors Bureau.

Restrictions: Dogs must be leashed and are not allowed in public buildings.

For more information: Denver Metro Convention and Visitors Bureau.

Getting started: The walk starts at the Denver Metro Convention and Visitors Bureau at 225 West Colfax Avenue. The center is easily accessible from Interstate 25 via the East Colfax Avenue exit.

Public transportation: An RTD bus station is on the north side of Civic Center Park, on Broadway. The Market Street Station is at the west end of the 16th Street Mall and offers connections to most areas of Denver. Call 303-299-6000 for schedules and route information.

Overview: In the heart of downtown Denver, Civic Center Park is the best place to begin any exploration of Colorado's largest city. Numerous points of interest surround the three-square-block park, downtown's largest, including three of Denver's "must-see" attractions—the U.S. Mint, the Denver Art Museum, and the Colorado State Capitol. By beginning your walking adventures here, you can do some sightseeing, become acquainted with Denver's public transportation system, pick up additional information at the Convention and Visitors Bureau, and discover some of the city's colorful history.

Civic Center Park is located just south of the downtown business district and its soaring skyscrapers. The park is an oasis of green grass and marvelous flower beds in summer, and holds an interesting assortment of statuary and monuments. It is bounded on the north by East Colfax Avenue, a main east-west thoroughfare, and on the south by 14th Avenue. The major north-south streets, Broadway and Lincoln Street, intersect at the park on its east side below the state capitol.

This 1-mile walk passes numerous state and local government buildings, as well as Museum Row on the park's south side, then explores the State Capitol, and finishes with a walk through the park. The route begins and ends at the Denver Metro Convention and Visitors Bureau on West Colfax Avenue. It's an easy walk on mostly level sidewalks with a short climb into the Capitol itself. This is a good walk for children, with lots of diversions and amusements.

of interest

The U.S. Mint

The Denver Branch of the U.S. Mint began as a private coin company in Denver's early gold mining days. It was later purchased by the federal government and eventually became a federal mint in 1895, pressing gold and silver coins. The five-story Gothic Renaissance building was built over five years beginning in 1897 with granite quarried along the Arkansas River and near Loveland. Marble from Tennessee and Vermont trims the building, while the perimeter wall is laid with pink Pikes Peak granite. Today the heavily guarded mint is the nation's second largest gold depository, after Fort Knox. It produces more than 5 billion coins annually, including more than 4 billion pennies that bear the "D" stamp.

The mint offers free tours on a first-come, first-served basis every fifteen to twenty minutes from the entrance on Cherokee Street. The tours are conducted weekdays from 8 A.M. to 2:45 P.M. Children under fourteen must be accompanied by an adult. The tour is not wheelchair-accessible.■

Parents should use judgment and restraint when taking kids into various buildings and museums along the way. The walk is also accessible to people with physical handicaps.

The walk

➤Begin at the Denver Metro Convention and Visitors Bureau at 225 West Colfax. Sitting on a small triangular block across from the City and County Building, the bureau offers a large assortment of visitor information, brochures, and maps, as well as a small gift shop. The staff is helpful and well-informed.

Although it is not part of this walking tour, the Denver Firefighters Museum sits one block west of the Convention and Visitors Bureau at 1326 Tremont Place. Located in Denver's Old Station No. 1, the museum preserves and displays early firefighting equipment and memorabilia, including two fire engines from the 1920s and some items dating from 1866.

➤From the Convention and Visitors Bureau, head south across busy Colfax Ave. at the crosswalk. To your right, across Cherokee Street, looms the imposing, monolithic U.S. Mint, one of Denver's most popular and beloved tourist attractions.

➤After leaving the mint, cross to the east side of Cherokee and head south (right) to 14th Avenue. Turn left.

To the left rears the Denver City and County Building, a prominent Denver landmark that houses local governmental offices. One of the last granite structures built in Denver, the grand building was meant to complement the Colorado State Capitol, which faces it on the east side of Civic Center Park. It was designed by thirty-nine Denver architects and completed in 1932 at a cost of almost $5 million. The east side of the building boasts a spectacular concave facade of Doric columns with a wide flight of granite stairs that rise to six 50-foot-high portico columns carved from Georgia granite. A flying eagle tops the ornate clock tower atop the building. The building is simply stunning from late November through December, when more than twenty thousand colored lights transform it into the world's largest Christmas lighting display. It's a Denver holiday tradition to bundle up and crunch through the snow around the building to eye the glittering lights.

➤Continue east on 14th Ave., crossing the street, then cross Bannock Street.

A block farther south is the Byers-Evans House. This historic house, at 1310 Bannock St. behind the art museum, was originally built in 1883 for *Rocky Mountain News* founder William N. Byers, who started Denver's first newspaper in 1859, a scant six days after arriving in the frontier town. He later sold the home to the son of John Evans, Colorado's second territorial governor. The house is now restored to the way it was from 1912 to 1924, with its original furnishings. Guided tours explore area history. The Denver History Museum, located in the house, details the city's past with exhibits and interactive video displays. Admission is charged.

➤From the corner of Bannock St. and 14th Ave., walk east on a sidewalk flanked on the right by a stone wall.

Above the sidewalk, the Denver Art Museum looms overhead like some futuristic castle. The twenty-eight-sided building, with its gleaming tiled exterior, was designed by Italian, Gio Ponti, and completed in 1971. It is sheathed with more than a million Corning glass tiles, each reflecting the sunlight. The six-floor museum houses more than 35 thousand pieces of art, including an acclaimed collection of Native American art and artifacts in its American Indian Hall. Highlights of this collection are totem poles, exquisite blankets, woven baskets, and Pueblo pottery. Other galleries house a contemporary collection including John DeAndrea's stunning lifelike sculpture Linda; pre-Columbian and Spanish Colonial art; classical European paintings; Western American art with works by Frederic Remington and Albert Bierstadt; African, Asian, and South Pacific art; and a marvelous folk-art textile collection featuring superb hand-stitched quilts.

The museum is open Tuesday through Saturday from 10 A.M. to 5 P.M. and Sunday from noon to 5 P.M. It's closed on Mondays and major holidays. Saturdays offer free admittance, while a nominal admission fee is charged during the rest of the week. The museum shop sells books, postcards, posters, toys, and folk art gifts. The museum's Great Works Cafe is a good place to stop for lunch or coffee after touring the galleries.

➤The walk continues on the tree-lined, cobbled sidewalk on the south side of 14th Ave. Directly across the street in the park is the 1919 Greek Theater, an outdoor amphitheater of granite constructed in classical Greek style. The open-air amphitheater has Ionic columns and tiers of stone seats, and is flanked by two stone lions.

The Denver Public Library lies just east of the art museum on the right side of 14th Ave. The huge library houses 5 million books, including one of the nation's largest collections of Western Americana. The library's main entrance is on Broadway, just south of 14th Ave.

➤The walk continues across Broadway, the main southbound thoroughfare in downtown Denver, via a pedestrian crosswalk. Continue east on 14th Ave.

The building between Broadway and Lincoln Street is the Colorado State Judicial Building. A unique set of steps rise to the open arch of the building. Walk up to the arch. Below you, visible through skylights, is the State Law Library. Above you stretches an upside-down, block-long mural painted by Angelo di Benedetto that depicts many famous lawgivers and peacemakers. It's fun to look up and pick out notable people, including Abraham Lincoln, Chief Ouray, and Martin Luther King Jr.

Immediately south of the judicial building is the Colorado History Museum with its long, angled north wall. The museum depicts Colorado's colorful history through dioramas of Native Americans, settlers, and miners; Native American and pioneer artifacts; mining relics and equipment; and historic photographs, including an excellent collection by famed photographer William Henry Jackson. A highlight is the 112-foot timeline that details 150 years of Colorado history. The museum also houses a comprehensive state research library, which is open to the public. A nominal admission fee is charged. The museum is open Monday through Saturday from 10 A.M. to 4:40 P.M. and Sundays from noon to 4:40 P.M.

➤From the east side of the judicial building, cross Lincoln Street, a major one-way, northbound street, then cross 14th Ave. again to its north side. From here the walk ascends a short hill east to the Colorado State Capitol. This gold-domed edifice was for years the focal point of Denver's skyline. Even today it stands apart from the city skyscrapers.

Walk up the sidewalks to the west side of the capitol. Climb the granite stairs to the building and note two often-photographed steps that say you are exactly "One Mile Above Sea Level." The first marker was placed in 1947. In 1969, however, engineering students from Colorado State University determined that the measurement was wrong, and a

of interest

The Colorado State Capitol

The state capitol is the seat of Colorado's government. It contains the legislative chambers for the House of Representatives and Senate as well as the governor's offices. Construction began on the building, designed in the same style as the nation's Capitol, in 1886 and was completed twenty-two years later. The building is made of granite excavated near Gunnison, Colorado, but the real treasure here is the priceless wainscoting of Colorado rose onyx marble that adorns the interior. The story of Colorado is told on a series of eight murals and poems on the first floor rotunda walls. Stained glass windows on the upper floors of the dome honor important Coloradoans—a hall of fame of sixteen pioneers who contributed to the state's early history including General William Jackson Palmer, Ute leader Chief Ouray, railroader Otto Mears, and newsman William Byers. The capitol dome, rising almost 300 feet from the ground, is plated with 200 ounces of tissue-thin gold leaf. The culmination of the walk is the trek up two spiral staircases and ninety-three steps to the base of the dome. An outside walkway offers excellent views of downtown Denver, Civic Center Park, and the Rocky Mountain skyline.■

geodetic survey plug was placed three steps higher at 5,280 feet—the exact mile-high altitude.

➤From the state capitol, head north (right) to Colfax Ave. then west (left) across Lincoln St. You will pass a Civil War memorial with two cannons and cavalryman. It honors Coloradoans who fought on the Union side in the War Between the States.

➤Upon reaching Lincoln St., walk a half-block north to a crosswalk and cross the street to the east end of Civic Center

Denver Civic Center.

Park. This grassy park section, occupying a square block between Lincoln and Broadway, has several war memorials. A red sandstone obelisk topped with a pointed beacon honors all of Colorado's war veterans. Nearby, the Joe P. Martinez Memorial is dedicated to Colorado's first Congressional Medal of Honor recipient in World War II. A replica of the Liberty Bell is found on the south side of the park.

➤At Broadway, cross at a pedestrian crosswalk to reach the bulk of Civic Center Park. Here, the walk meanders on paved sidewalks through the park. You'll see several striking statues, including Bucking Bronco and On The War Trail by sculptor Alexander Phimister Proctor. Colorful flower beds scatter across the park in late spring and summer. Originally covered with houses, the land that is now the park was cleared by Mayor Robert Speer in 1904 in an attempt to beautify downtown Denver.

The Voorhies Memorial, framed by Ionic columns and sea lion fountains, was built with money bequeathed by miner John H. P. Voorhies.

➤Finish the walk by continuing west through the park, past some formal flower gardens, to Bannock St. opposite the City and County Building. Turn right (north) on the east side of Bannock and walk to Colfax Ave. Cross Bannock at a crosswalk and walk on the south side of Colfax to reach the walk's endpoint opposite the Convention and Visitors Bureau.

Walk 2

16th Street Mall

General location: In the retail heart of downtown Denver, on a closed pedestrian mall that runs from Market Street to Broadway.

Special attractions: Tabor Center Shops, May D & F Tower, Writer's Square, Paramount Theater, many historic buildings, shopping, people-watching, outdoor cafes, microbreweries, and pubs.

Difficulty rating: Easy. A level route on sidewalks, the walk is barrier-free and suitable for small children in strollers or people in wheelchairs.

Distance: 1.3 to 2.6 miles, depending on whether you walk the mall one-way and take the free public shuttle back to your starting point or walk both up and down the mall.

Estimated time: 1.5 hours (round trip).

16th Street Mall

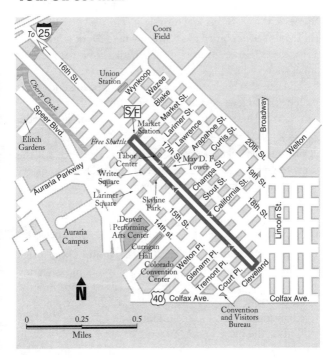

Services: All services are found along the mall, including restaurants, shops, restrooms, water fountains, telephones, and park benches.

Restrictions: Dogs must be leashed, and you must clean up their droppings. No motorized vehicles or bicycles.

For more information: Denver Metro Convention and Visitors Bureau.

Getting started: The walk begins and ends in downtown Denver. The easiest exit from Interstate 25 is Colfax Avenue.

Head east on Colfax to the downtown area and turn left onto North Speer Boulevard, a diagonal four-lane road. Follow Speer to Market Street and turn right. The walk begins at the RTD bus station on Market Street, where Market intersects 16th Street. Parking can be problematic. Look for metered street spots or parking lots en route to the bus terminal.

You can also begin the walk from the opposite end of the mall by starting at the Civic Center bus terminal on Broadway. Cross Broadway to the 16th Street Mall and follow the walking directions in reverse.

Public transportation: Local RTD bus service accesses the downtown area from all sections of Denver. A free courtesy shuttle bus follows 16th St. through the mall and stops at every block.

Overview: This walk explores the 16th Street Mall, a mile-long pedestrian mall that stretches along 16th St. from Broadway to Market Street. Renovated stone and brick buildings, outdoor cafes and superb restaurants, towering glass and steel skyscrapers, and hundreds of shops line the mall. Several parks, plazas, and eleven fountains are scattered amid the gray and red granite sidewalks.

This is the place in downtown Denver to people-watch. Every type and sort of Denverite can be found here: businesspeople dressed in chic fashions, panhandlers showing their handiwork, tourists wearing fanny packs and carrying city maps, and artists, musicians, and mimes performing for small change.

You can access the mall easily from anywhere in downtown Denver. Since regular free shuttle buses run the length of the mall every few minutes, you can do the walk in one of two ways. Either walk up one side of the mall and back down the other, or walk up the mall and ride on the shuttle back to your starting point.

Retail Row

16th Street has long been Denver's "Retail Row." Nearby Larimer Street and the surrounding blocks were Denver's first commercial district, but as the city grew, the business district expanded. Along Wynkoop Street and the railroad tracks was "Warehouse Row," home to the storage and manufacturing facilities of large Rocky Mountain wholesalers. After streetcars started plying 16th St. in the 1870s, many of the large merchants moved their stores there, and by the 1890s, the three big department stores—Joslin's, McNamara's, and Daniels & Fisher—were firmly established on 16th St.. In 1911, William C. Daniels built a lavish tower above his D & F store. Until 1953, it was Denver's tallest building.

On 16th St., customers could buy almost anything. Jerome Smiley wrote in 1901, "About all the needs and most of the fancies of men and women may be satisfied in the emporiums." It is still that way. Today's pedestrian shopping mall with a flourishing selection of diverse retailers and free shuttle buses was completed in 1982 at a cost of $76 million. The mall is a tree-lined, walker-friendly promenade that runs through the vibrant heart of downtown Denver.■

The walk

➤The walk begins at the Regional Transportation District (RTD) Market Street Station at the far northwest end of the 16th Street Mall. Surrounded by a concrete plaza with benches and sculptures, the station serves several RTD routes. The RTD administrative office building, at 1600

Blake, sits adjacent to the plaza in what was originally the 1882 David Creswell Brass Foundry. Buses from around the metro area empty at the station in an underground bus terminal. Free shuttle buses run up and down the 16th Street Mall from the station.

➤Cross Market St. southeast of the station and walk southeast along the closed street which is the 16th Street Mall.

➤After one block cross Larimer Street. Denver's first commercial thoroughfare, Larimer St. arose during Denver's early days when William Larimer platted the townsite as a rival to Auraria, on the opposite side of Cherry Creek. Larimer Square, a couple of blocks southwest, is a renovated, one-block historic district centered around Larimer St. Designated as Denver's first historic district in 1973, the square preserves ten historic buildings that are now filled with galleries, shops, and restaurants (see Walk 3).

➤Continue walking along the mall. The Tabor Center, a huge, airy retail center built in 1985, straddles the left side of the two blocks between Larimer and Arapahoe streets, along with an adjoining office center and the Westin Hotel. Stop and browse in the glass-enclosed galleria. Inside are plant-lined walkways leading to more than sixty-five restaurants and shops, including B.Dalton Booksellers, Crabtree & Evelyn, The Sharper Image, Contempo Casuals, and The Toy Corner. A covered glass bridge spans Lawrence Street between the center's two buildings, offering a changing selection of vendors' carts.

On the opposite side of the mall from the Tabor Center between Larimer and Lawrence streets is Writer's Square. This block of brick buildings houses numerous shops and restaurants on its ground level with offices and condominium lofts above.

The mall block between Lawrence and Arapahoe streets has a few Denver landmark buildings. The Central Bank building (1515 Arapahoe), constructed in 1973 by Muchow & Associates, is an award-winning building that was part of Denver's Skyline Redevelopment Project. The Daniels & Fisher (D & F) Tower, on the corner of 16th and Arapahoe, is one of the Mile High City's most famous and recognizable architectural landmarks. The 372-foot tower, erected in 1911, was the tallest building west of the Mississippi River and the third tallest in the United States at the time of its construction—but only if you counted the height of its flagpole. The cream-colored tower, with four clocks and a 5,000-pound bell, loomed over William C. Daniels's five-story department store, one of Denver's finest marts.

Built in Renaissance Revival style, the tower was modeled after the 700-year-old campanile of St. Mark's Basilica in Venice, Italy, which Daniels had seen while visiting Europe. At the same time it was being constructed, its Italian counterpart collapsed and was rebuilt, leading the *Denver Post* to boast "Venetians Erecting a Column—Almost Exact Replica of D & F's Tower in Denver." Until the department store closed in 1958, visitors could ride an elevator to a twentieth-floor observation deck and souvenir shop.

In 1953, the Mile High Center surpassed the tower as the city's tallest building, and by the 1980s it was lost below a maze of skyscrapers. The D & F Tower narrowly escaped the bulldozers of the Urban Renewal Authority, which leveled the rest of the store. During the tower's 1981 restoration, workers found an urn hidden in the walls; it contained the ashes of William C. Daniels. The tower is now a beloved symbol of historic Denver, but it is no longer open to the public.

On the opposite side of 16th St. from the D & F Tower is one of the Skyline Parks. These three 1-acre parks rim the west edge of Arapahoe St. between 15th and 18th streets. In summer you can sit beside a gurgling fountain or under a shady tree here and watch Denver walk by.

➤Continue along the mall to Curtis Street. On the corner is the Rock Bottom Brewery, where you can enjoy lunch and hand-crafted beers on an outside patio, fronting the mall. A double-decker British bus, parked at the northeast corner of Curtis and 16th, sells tickets for local performances, lotteries, and buses, and provides information on daily mall events.

On the opposite (southeast) corner is Joslin's Department Store, founded by merchandiser John Jay Joslin in 1873. The building's original exterior was plastered over in the 1950s.

A couple of blocks down Curtis St. to the right (southwest) sits the Denver Performing Arts Complex with Boettcher Concert Hall, the Helen Bonfils Theatre Complex, and the Denver Auditorium Theatre.

➤Cross Curtis St. and walk up 16th St. to Champa Street. Midway up the block on the south side of 16th is the twelve-story University Building. Built in 1910, it now houses shops and restaurants. The elegant brick building was the A. C. Foster Building until the University of Denver bought it. The Kortz Clock in front of the building is the only pedestrian obstacle on the entire mall.

➤Cross Champa St. On the right side of the street is the 1906 Symes Building (820 16th St.). This was the site of Judge George G. Symes's house until 1880, when he built the first Symes Building, which burned down in 1905. The following year a new, grander building with detailed ornamentation was constructed. It was the first steel frame structure in Denver, and was later converted into "the world's largest" Woolworth store.

Farther up 16th St. is the 1891 Holzman–Appel Block (808 16th St.), which long housed a department store. Note the Romanesque Revival architectural details on the upper floors.

On the southeast corner of 16th and Champa is the Champa Center. The center, a renovated Sears store, offers a food court with fast food restaurants, shops, and offices. Two blocks down Champa St. to the southwest is the Currigan Exhibition Hall, site of trade shows and expositions.

➤Continue walking on 16th St., crossing Stout Street. On the south side of 16th is the five-story Neusteters Department Store (720 16th St.). Built in 1924 as an addition to the original 1911 store founded by Max and Meyer Neusteter, it is described in the book *Denver, The City Beautiful* as an effort "to balance classical horizontal lines with modern vertical trends." Inside, Colorado muralist Vance Kirkland painted five murals depicting beauty and culture. The store closed in 1985. Now numerous shops are located on its ground floor, with four floors of condominiums above.

Farther up 16th is the Denver Dry Building (700 16th St.). This elegantly appointed brick building, designed by famed Denver architect Frank E. Edbrooke, once housed the Denver Dry Goods Company, one of Denver's largest department stores. The company began on Larimer St. as McNamara's Dry Goods Company before it moved to 16th St. just before the silver-based Panic of 1893. An 1894 bank foreclosure led to the store being reorganized as the Denver Dry Goods Co. It closed its doors in 1987 after its rival May D & F (now Foley's) bought it. A 1990s renovation reopened the old store building, with new shops and offices inside.

May D&F Tower on the 16th Street Mall walk.

The Colorado Building (1615 California St.) is across 16th St. from the Denver Dry Building. This interesting edifice began as the Hayden, Dickinson, & Feldman Building in 1891. Over the next few decades it was remodeled and refaced in a variety of eclectic styles, notably Art Deco in a 1935 facelift. This ornate look was crowned by white terra cotta peaks along the roofline. Between the first and second floors, note the bas-relief fir trees on a long strip of terra cotta.

➤Cross California St. and continue southeast on the mall. The Steele Building (616 16th St.), on the right, was a Steele Department Store when it opened in 1922. More than one hundred thousand customers came on opening day, but the store closed three months later along with the entire chain of ninety-nine Steele stores (a classic case of too much too soon).

➤Cross Welton Street. The block between Welton and Glenarm boasts a couple of Denver's best historic buildings, the Masonic Temple and the Kittredge Building. The Masonic Temple, on the corner of 16th and Welton, is one of the last sandstone buildings still standing in downtown Denver. The 1889 building, built with blocks of ruddy Manitou sandstone from the Colorado Springs area, was designed by famed Denver architect (and Mason) Frank Edbrooke. The five-story building was almost destroyed by a huge fire set by a disgruntled tenant in 1984. A careful restoration saved the exterior, and a new steel framework was erected inside the thick stone walls to create today's retail and office space. Check out the exquisite stone carving on the 15-foot-wide arch spanning the Welton St. entrance.

The Kittredge Building (511 16th St.) is as interesting as its neighbor. This seven-story edifice, built from Colorado granite and rhyolite, was built in 1891. Note the stone arch and columns, the large Pikes Peak granite blocks on the lower two stories, and the elaborate carvings on the upper cornices and turrets along the roofline.

Next door, on the corner of 16th St. and Glenarm Place, resides the 2,100-seat Paramount Theatre. The last of Denver's old-time movie theaters, this classic theater has an Art Deco interior topped by a grand chandelier. Its dual-console Wurlitzer pipe organ is one of only two left in the country.

➤Cross Glenarm Place and continue up 16th St. to Tremont St. Here, the Republic Plaza Tower, with fifty-six skyscraping stories, is Denver's tallest building. It is only 9 inches below the maximum height for Denver buildings allowed by the Federal Aviation Administration. The spacious plaza below the tower makes a good place to stop and rest, offering granite benches below shady trees.

Across 16th St. are two buildings designed by the famous architect I. M. Pei—the May D & F Department Store (350 16th St.) and the nearby Radisson Hotel (1550 Court Place). Both were built in 1958.

➤Continue up 16th, crossing Court St., and end your walk at Broadway, one of Denver's primary north-south routes. From here you can retrace your steps back down the mall to Market Street Station or take the free shuttle bus back to your starting point. Or, if you wish, cross Broadway to the RTD Civic Center bus terminal.

Walk 3

Historic Lower Downtown

General location: Historic Lower Downtown (LoDo), just northwest of Denver's skyscrapers.

Special attractions: Writer's Square, Larimer Square Historic District, Lower Downtown Historic District, Union Station, many historic buildings and warehouses, brew pubs, Coors Field.

Difficulty rating: Easy. Following flat sidewalks with curb cuts, the walk is barrier-free and suitable for small children, babies in strollers, and people in wheelchairs.

Distance: 1.5 miles

Estimated time: 1 hour.

Historic Lower Downtown

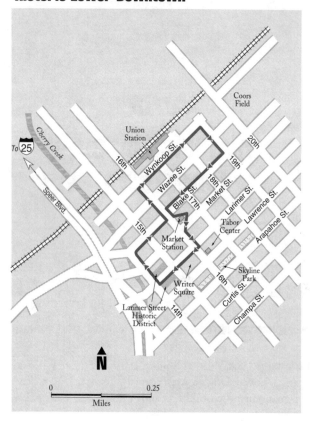

Services: All services are found along the walk, including galleries, shops, and an excellent selection of restaurants.

Restrictions: None. The walk is wheelchair-accessible. Traffic is usually moderate, and all intersections are easy to cross. Dogs must be leashed. Carry plastic bags to clean up after your pet.

For more information: Denver Metro Convention and Visitors Bureau.

Getting started: This walk begins at the Regional Transportation District (RTD) Market Street Station at the west end of the 16th Street Mall. The station is readily accessed by RTD buses from all over the metro area. Both the 16th Street Mall and station are easy to reach from Interstate 25 via either the Colfax Avenue or Speer Boulevard exits. If arriving by car, look for on-street, metered parking or plentiful private parking lots near the station and in Lower Downtown.

Public transportation: Several RTD bus routes stop at the Market Street Station.

Overview: This walk explores historic Larimer Square, Denver's first designated historic district, and Lower Downtown (LoDo). LoDo was Denver's warehouse district from the time that the railroad arrived here in 1870 until the end of World War II. Numerous excellent and well-preserved buildings line the sidewalks here, offering you a glimpse into Denver's colorful past.

Larimer Square, centered around a single block of Larimer St., preserves a slice of old Denver. Once a part of Denver's infamous red-light district, with saloons, brothels, flophouses, and casinos, the renovated square now houses numerous chic shops and great restaurants.

LoDo, Denver's "Skid Row" during harder times, is another exciting and rejuvenated part of old Denver near the railroad tracks. At one time, huge mercantile companies stored and sold their myriad goods from the immense brick warehouses that tower above its busy streets. Distribution and manufacturing empires that spread across the West were headquartered in its edifices. Now these same streets house more than sixty restaurants, coffee shops, and brew pubs, along with numerous art galleries, an excellent bookstore, and Coors Field, home of the Colorado Rockies National League baseball team.

The walk

➤Start at the RTD Market Street Station (Market and 16th St.) at the far northwest end of the 16th Street Mall. Surrounded by a concrete plaza with benches and sculptures, the station is one of downtown Denver's main RTD hubs. Buses from around the metro area empty here in an underground bus terminal. Free shuttle buses run up and down the 16th Street Mall.

➤From the station, cross Market Street to the east and walk a block southeast on the 16th Street Mall to Larimer Street.

➤Cross Larimer St. and turn right. Walk a block to 15th Street. On the southeast side of Larimer is Writer's Square, a 1981 development filled with restaurants, shops, offices, and condominiums. It is worth a visit.

➤Cross 15th St. and enter the Larimer Street Historic District. With false-fronted buildings and wooden sidewalks, Larimer St. was born in 1858 when William Larimer staked a gold claim on nearby Cherry Creek. Within a decade this street changed dramatically as brick commercial buildings began lining the dusty lane. Photographs from those early days depict a block that appears almost as it does today, with two- and three-story buildings. The nineteenth-century scene was colored by rows of striped awnings that shaded the sidewalk, and by painted signs that advertised wallpaper, smokers' articles, Singer sewing machines, a drug store, and a photographic studio.

Over the years, Larimer St. slowly degenerated into a seedy red-light district with brothels, casinos, and as many as fifty-seven saloons. By the 1970s, Denver's Urban Renewal Authority threatened to bulldoze the area, but citizens protested, and the 1400 block of Larimer was designated Denver's first historic district in 1973. Larimer Square was renovated and restored to its former splendor. It now boasts a selection of almost thirty trendy shops and galleries, ten chic restaurants and coffee shops, and its own microbrewery, Champion Brewing Company.

►Continue walking southwest down the 1400 block of Larimer through the heart of the historic district. On the corner, at 1460 Larimer, is the Clayton Building and former Granite Hotel, an 1882 stone building erected on the site of William Larimer's 1858 log cabin. At 1426 Larimer is the 1873 Kettle Building, the oldest edifice in Larimer Square. The first floor of this narrow, 20-foot-wide building was removed in 1990 to create an arched passageway that leads to a rear courtyard with shops and the Little Russian Cafe. Step into the corridor and look up at a mural of early Denverites painted on the vaulted ceiling.

The west side of the street also has some interesting buildings. The three-story brick Gallup-Stanbury Building at 1445-1451 Larimer was originally the Tambien Saloon. The two-story Crawford Building at 1439 Larimer is a spectacular example of the Second Empire style. Built in 1875, the building has exquisite detailing that includes cast iron columns and an ornate metal frieze and parapet. The 1887 Lincoln Hall at 1413 Larimer began as a noisy dance hall with a springy floor suspended from cables before becoming a harness shop.

On the corner of Larimer and 14th streets was the infamous saloon of city councilman John Gahan Sr. Politicians would stop by for a drink after exiting the old 1883 City Hall, which stood across 14th on a site now marked by the old city hall bell. The hall was demolished in the 1940s. A shop now sells women's clothes in the bar space where grog was once poured.

➤From the corner of Larimer and 14th, turn right (northwest) onto 14th St. Views to Mount Evans in the snowcapped Front Range fill the horizon above the Auraria Campus of the University of Colorado at Denver on the other side of Cherry Creek (see Walk 4).

➤Cross Market St. and continue along 14th St. until it curves right onto Blake Street, where you enter the Lower Downtown Historic District, affectionately dubbed "LoDo" by locals.

➤Follow Blake Street for two blocks to the 16th Street Mall. You'll pass several points of interest along the way.

Constitution Hall, a brick building on the corner at 1501 Blake, stands on the location of the Colorado Constitutional Convention in the winter of 1875-76. The original hall was torched by an arsonist in 1977.

The Barney Ford Building, at 1514 Blake, housed Barney Ford's People's Restaurant after the great Denver fire of 1863 wiped out his original saloon and barbershop. Ford was a former slave who escaped the South via the Underground Railroad. After making his way to Chicago, he traveled west

LoDo

The Lower Downtown Historic District was a bustling commercial and mercantile district during its heyday in the late nineteenth century. The Union Pacific railroad, arriving in Denver on June 15, 1870, brought new businesses and goods for booming Colorado Territory and its growing population. LoDo, surrounding the Denver railroad yards and stations, expanded into a huge warehouse and business area. Massive brick buildings, many adorned with fine architectural details, were erected on its busy streets.

After the Panic of 1893, Denver's fortunes dwindled, and by the 1940s the LoDo area was on a downward spiral. The trucking industry and the interstate highway system dealt a severe economic blow to the railroad-based district, and much of the area was scheduled for demolition. The 1970s revival of neighboring Larimer Square led preservationists and developers to buy and renovate much of the old warehouse district. In 1988, LoDo's unique historical value led to its designation as a Denver Historic District.

Today the rejuvenated Lower Downtown, bounded on the southeast by Market Street and on the northwest by Wynkoop Street and the railroad tracks, is a thriving business and retail center. More than sixty restaurants, brew pubs, coffee shops, and taverns scatter across the area's nineteen square blocks, including the Wynkoop Brewing Company, Colorado's first brew pub. An eclectic assortment of more than forty art galleries sells artworks of all types, from Southwestern to African to contemporary. LoDo's many shops include the Tattered Cover Bookstore, with more than 500,000 volumes. Coors Field, home of the National League's Colorado Rockies baseball team, anchors the northeast side of LoDo on 20th Street. The area surrounding the baseball field is jammed with sports bars, restaurants, and more brew pubs.■

in 1860 and became Denver's most prominent black settler. The building was remodeled and enlarged in the 1890s to its present state.

The 1400 block between Blake and Wazee streets is known as the Elephant Corral. The first building erected here was a crude log cabin, built in 1858 by Charles Blake and Andrew Williams. Flanked by a corral, it was a popular stop for emigrants, allowing them to water and feed their stock and trade oxen for sure-footed mules for mountain travel. The cabin evolved into the Denver Hotel, an inn for newcomers that welcomed, among others, newspaperman Horace Greeley in 1859. The hotel burned in the Great Fire of 1863, and from its ashes rose a brick warehouse. Over the decades, the various buildings on the block were torn down, altered, and remodeled. Now the area is a ritzy office complex.

➤At 16th and Blake, turn left, cross Blake, and walk along 16th St. for two blocks, passing Wazee St. and reaching Wynkoop St.

The Sugar Building, at 1530 16th St., is on the corner of Wazee and 16th. This building was erected in 1906 as the headquarters of the Great Western Sugar Company. Note the terra cotta decorations on the moldings and cornices. Inside the lobby is the oldest working Otis elevator west of the Mississippi River.

Across the road at 1545 Wazee is the Henry Lee Building. Lee, an agriculturist and one of the founders of Denver's city park system, had the warehouse constructed in 1886 for his farm implement business. It was later connected to the Morey Mercantile Building, across the alley, and used as a spice mill, peanut butter factory, and coffee roasting plant. Note the double-wide alley off 16th St., which allowed railroad access to loading docks behind the warehouses.

Union Station on the Lower Downtown walk.

The Chester S. Morey Mercantile Building, on the corner of 16th and Wynkoop, was built in 1896 for $75,000. Reputedly one of Denver's most elegant warehouses, it was headquarters for Morey's flourishing mercantile business and boasted 253,000 square feet by 1925. The company made and sold a wide range of goods, including jams and jellies, cigars, stationery, snuff, brooms, and Solitarie brand coffee, and was the largest wholesaler in the Rocky Mountains until 1956. Morey later acquired the Great Western Sugar Company. His immense brick edifice is now home to the Tattered Cover Bookstore, one of Denver's largest bookshops with more than 500,000 volumes.

➤At the corner of 16th and Wynkoop streets, go right (northeast) along Wynkoop. Once nicknamed "Warehouse Row," Wynkoop St. was the center of Denver's booming warehouse and storage district. Numerous old warehouses, ranging from three to five stories in height, line the street and face the railyard. All were made out of brick in simple, functional designs.

➤Walk along Wynkoop for three blocks to 19th Street. Note the bronze street names inlaid in the sidewalks.

The most impressive landmark on Wynkoop is the fabulous Union Station at 17th Street. Opened in 1881, this depot consolidated eight separate depots. The grand station, designed in Italian Romanesque style, was constructed from rhyolite blocks and trimmed in sandstone. For a time, it was Colorado's largest building. Though an 1894 fire destroyed the station's 180-foot tower, the main section was rebuilt and later remodeled to its present style with granite blocks and elaborate terra cotta decorations. During the railroad heyday, more than a million passengers a year and up to eighty trains a day passed through Union Station. Now only one or two trains stop each day. The depot's basement houses one of the country's largest model railroad exhibits. Check inside to find out when it is open to the public.

Other buildings along Wynkoop include the Denver City Railway Building (1635 17th St.), the J. S. Brown Mercantile Building (1792 Wynkoop), the Littleton Creamery (1801 Wynkoop), and the Union Pacific Freight House (1735 19th St.). The Brown Mercantile housed the offices and warehouse of one of Denver's first wholesale businesses. The company started in 1861 and was bought out by its main competitor, Morey Mercantile, in 1937. Now the building is home to Wynkoop Brewing Co., Colorado's first brew pub. It makes a good stop for a tankard of Railroad Ale. The freight house, sitting on 19th just west of Wynkoop, is a superb brick Neoclassical building with dual Colonial columns flanking the front door.

➤Turn right onto 19th Street. To the left, beyond a parking lot, towers Coors Field, the home of the Colorado Rockies baseball club. The stadium, erected in 1995, is an old-style ballpark that fits into the historic warehouse district with its brick facing, arched entrance, and terra cotta details.

➤Continue up 19th and cross Wazee St. The 1931 Merchandise Mart, on the corner, was the last building constructed in LoDo until its 1980s rejuvenation. The brick building now offers condominium housing.

➤At the junction of 19th and Blake streets, turn right onto Blake. Numerous shops and restaurants line the street, offering pleasant diversions. Interesting buildings are the Crocker Cracker Factory (1862 Blake), Windsor Dairy (1855 Blake), and the Carter Rice Building (1623 Blake). The cracker factory was built in 1887 as a steam cracker bakery. It was renovated in 1983 into office and retail space. The Windsor Dairy operated here from 1918 until 1929.

Meadow Gold bought it out and ran the dairy operation until 1973.

➤ Follow Blake for three blocks to the 16th Street Mall and the Market Street RTD station. Step left to the station and the end of the walk.

Walk 4

Old Auraria

General location: On the historic Auraria Campus of the University of Colorado at Denver, Metropolitan State College, and the Community College of Denver, just west of downtown.

Special attractions: Denver Performing Arts Complex, St. Elizabeth's Church, Ninth Street Historic District, St. Cajetan's Church, old Tivoli Brewery, and Cherry Creek.

Difficulty rating: Easy. Paved sidewalks throughout, with curb cuts allowing access for people in wheelchairs.

Distance: 2 miles.

Estimated time: 1 hour.

Services: Food, drink, and restrooms are found on the Auraria Campus. Check out the Mercantile Restaurant and the Tivoli Student Union.

Old Auraria

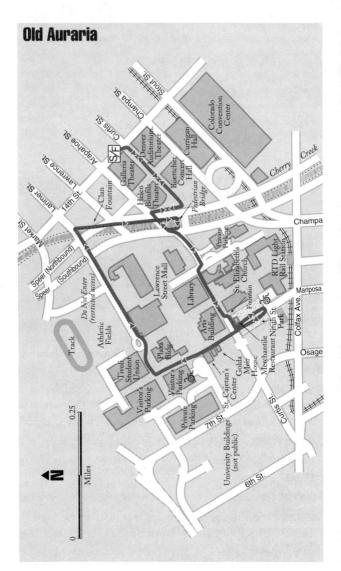

Restrictions: Dogs must be leashed.

For more information: Denver Metro Convention and Visitors Bureau.

Getting started: The walk begins at the Denver Performing Arts Complex on the west side of the intersection of Curtis and 14th streets. From Interstate 25, find the starting point by taking either the Speer Boulevard exit or the Colfax Avenue exit. From the Speer exit, drive southeast into downtown Denver. Turn left onto Lawrence Street and drive one block to 14th Street. Turn right on 14th, drive two blocks to the intersection of 14th and Curtis streets, and find on-street metered parking or park in one of the nearby garages. From the Colfax exit, go east toward the state capitol, and turn left on Speer. Drive four blocks to Lawrence and follow the directions above. The start is only two blocks southwest of the 16th Street Mall.

Public transportation: Downtown Denver is served by Regional Transportation District (RTD) buses as well as light rail. RTD stations are at either end of the 16th Street Mall. Ride the free mall shuttle to Curtis St.

Overview: The western bank of Cherry Creek, a placid stream that flows from the Palmer Divide south of Denver, is the site of Auraria, one of the area's first settlements. An expedition of Georgia prospectors, led by William Greeneberry Russell, arrived here in 1858 and found specks of gold in Cherry Creek. To protect their placers, the men founded Auraria City that autumn, naming their fledgling village after their Georgia hometown and a Latin word for gold. They then promptly went east for the winter, leaving a handful of miners bivouacked in tents, tepees, and crude log cabins.

That same winter, promoter William Larimer founded Denver on the opposite bank of Cherry Creek, naming his town after Kansas Territorial Governor James Denver. Larimer and his group staked out streets, sold lots to newcomers, and made a bundle of money. That spring, prospector George Jackson uncovered color at Idaho Springs; in May, John Gregory found Colorado's first vein of lode gold near today's Central City. Almost overnight, miners stampeded to what was dubbed "the richest square mile on earth." Most of them passed through Denver and Auraria. The rival towns vied for their attention, but Denver became top dog when the Smoky Hill stagecoach line arrived in 1859. In April 1860, Auraria quietly merged with Denver, becoming a residential and industrial suburb.

More than a hundred years later, Denver's Urban Renewal Authority began to demolish much of downtown Denver. Most of old Auraria was razed to make way for the Auraria Higher Education Center, a 171-acre campus that is now part of the University of Colorado at Denver, Metropolitan State College, and the Community College of Denver. Local preservationists, including Historic Denver, Inc. and the Denver Landmark Preservation Commission, were able to save some of the area's notable buildings and houses. This walk explores the remaining historic buildings on the Auraria Campus as well as the nearby Denver Performing Arts Complex.

The walk

►Begin at the Denver Performing Arts Complex on the west side of the intersection of Curtis and 14th streets. Walk west under the immense, arched Galleria that connects the old Denver Auditorium Theatre with the Helen Bonfils Theatre Complex and a multi-story parking garage. This

Under the arcade at the Performing Arts Center.

vaulting arcade, roofed with clear plastic and open at either end, offers a superb view west to the Front Range.

The Denver Performing Arts Complex, nicknamed "The PLEX," is the second largest theater complex in the nation, surpassed only by New York's Lincoln Center. Its nine theaters offer a wide variety of entertainment, including opera, symphony, theater, and dance. Of particular note is Boettcher Concert Hall, with its unique symphony-in-the-round staging—it's home to the Denver Symphony Orchestra.

The grand edifice on your left is the Denver Municipal Auditorium. This beige brick Neoclassical building, trimmed in terra cotta, opened on July 4, 1908, for the Democratic National Convention (to date the only presidential convention ever held in Denver). The 12,000-seat hall was second in size only to Madison Square Garden at the time of its construction.

The 2,800-seat Temple Hoyne Buell Theater, built in 1991, opens from the auditorium to the Galleria. The Buell Theater was named after a prominent Denver architect and philanthropist. Continue west in the Galleria to *Infinite Energy*, an unusual sculpture created by Victor Contreras from Cuernavaca, Mexico. Boettcher Concert Hall flanks the left side of the Galleria, while the Helen Bonfils Theater Complex, with four theaters, sits on the right. It houses the Denver Center Theater Company, the largest resident theater company in the Rocky Mountain West.

➤At the west end of the Galleria, descend steps or a wheelchair ramp onto a plaza. Keep right and descend more steps or another ramp to the level of Speer Boulevard.

➤Keep right on sidewalks to the crossing lights at the intersection of Arapahoe Street and Speer Blvd. Cross north over Arapahoe at the crosswalk and then go west across Speer

Blvd. at the crosswalk. Speer is divided by Cherry Creek into north and southbound lanes.

➤On the west side of Speer, stop and get your bearings. The walk now proceeds southwest toward St. Elizabeth's Catholic Church, a prominent spired church. Follow paved sidewalks toward the church and the Auraria Campus. The 171-acre Auraria Higher Education Center, a commuter campus, is shared by three Denver schools—the University of Colorado at Denver, Metropolitan State College, and the Community College of Denver. The schools share classrooms, office space, and administrative services.

St. Elizabeth's Catholic Church, home to an active parish, was erected in 1898 as the centerpiece of early Denver's large German Catholic community. The parish was founded twenty years earlier by immigrants. The church was built with rough-cut blocks of rhyolite from Castle Rock, a volcanic deposit south of Denver. It boasts a lofty spire that soars 162 feet above the sandstone front steps. On its south is St. Elizabeth's Monastery, which once connected the church to a convent and parish school and now abuts the modern St. Francis Conference Center.

➤Walk west from St. Elizabeth's toward the campus library along a wide sidewalk flanked by benches and bike racks. Go under a bridge that connects the Arts and West Classroom buildings. Continue onto a brick sidewalk past a round, iron horse trough dating from 1898.

➤At the corner with the Mercantile Building, now a student deli, turn left (south) onto a brick and stone sidewalk and enter the 9th Street Park Historic District. As you walk south, note the sandstone curbs from the old street, which is now covered by lawn.

The 9th Street Park Historic District, listed on the National Register of Historic Places, is a one-block area of superb Victorian cottages preserved in their original style and now used as college offices. This area of Denver was once residential, its streets lined with modest frame and brick houses. Denver's oldest district, Auraria was settled in the late 1850s. The arrival of the railroad changed the neighborhood, adding warehouses, industrial buildings, and shops. After a long downward turn, the Denver Urban Renewal Authority began bulldozing the district in the 1970s to make way for the Auraria Campus. Preservationists were able to salvage some of the area's architectural gems, including three churches, the Tivoli Brewery, and this full block of homes on 9th Street. These fourteen homes and one store were built between 1872 and 1906. Interpretive signs along the sidewalk at each home describe the area's architecture and colorful history.

The Mercantile Restaurant was once the Groussman Grocery. The two-story building was erected in 1906 and operated by Albert Groussman, who lived upstairs.

The Italianate-style house at 1061 Ninth is one of the oldest on the block, dating from 1874.

At the end of the block is the Knight House, 1015 Ninth. This charming house, built in 1885, was the home of miller Stephen Knight. In his book *Auraria: Where Denver Began*, Don Etter calls it "perhaps the most perfectly proportioned and tastefully embellished Victorian house in Denver."

➤At the end of the block, turn right on the sidewalk and walk west to the opposite side of Ninth. Walk north on the sidewalk along the west side of the street. The oldest house on this block is the Smedley House (1020 Ninth), a lovely frame residence built in 1872 before city regulations required brick construction for fire prevention. It was originally erected on the edge of the prairie by dentist William Smedley. In 1947 it became Casa Mayan, a popular Mexican restaurant run by Ramon and Caroline Gonzales, who lived upstairs with their seven children. The restaurant closed in 1973.

➤Continue north from the historic district along the sidewalk. At the end of this block, on the left, is the Golda Meir House, the teenage home of the woman who became Israel's prime minister. Russian-born Golda Meir, then named Golda Mabovitch, moved to Denver in 1914 and attended North High School. After her 1917 wedding to Morris Myerson, she moved to Palestine. The red brick house, a meeting place for Denver's Jewish residents, was originally located on Julian Street in "Little Israel" and was moved here to avoid demolition.

➤Walk north on Ninth to the plaza in front of St. Cajetan's Catholic Church. This gorgeous old church, now a campus performing arts center, was built in the Spanish Colonial style in 1926. The stucco church looks like a country church from old Mexico, with twin bell towers, round arches, and a red tile roof. Local flour magnate John Mullen donated his house, which once occupied the site, and $50,000 toward the church's construction. Its mostly Hispanic parish relocated to a new church in 1975.

➤Continue north for a block, between classroom buildings, to reach the old Tivoli Brewery. Turn right onto the brick sidewalk and courtyard at the southwest corner of the building. The Tivoli Brewery, now the Tivoli Student Union, is a large white-and-blue brick building that covers one square block. Denver's first brewery, the Rocky Mountain Brewery was started in 1859 by German immigrant John Goode, opened for business on this site in 1881 and gradually expanded with adjoining buildings. Goode named his brewery after the Tivoli Gardens in Copenhagen, Denmark. In 1900 it became the Tivoli-Union Brewery, which brewed its delectable beverages until it closed in 1969. During the 1980s, it was a retail mall. In 1991, Auraria Campus students voted to make the old brewery their new student center. Restrooms, snacks, and coffee are available inside.

➤Walk northeast on the sidewalk to the terminus of Larimer Street. Continue down the brick sidewalk on the right side of Larimer. You will pass the Physical Education Center, then the glass-and-steel North Classroom Building, the largest higher education building in Colorado. Playing fields occupy the area north of Larimer St.

➤Cross Speer Boulevard and Cherry Creek at the lighted crosswalk.

➤On the east side of Speer Blvd., locate the set of stairs or wheelchair ramp that descend to a pedestrian path alongside Cherry Creek. The Clan Fountain's colorful steel figures sit in a plaza alongside the creek. The fountain offers a peaceful respite from the busy streets above.

➤Walk left (south) on the concrete sidewalk along the east bank of Cherry Creek. The west bank is reserved for bicyclists; the east bank is for walkers.

➤Continue along the Cherry Creek viaduct. A plaque recalls a warning the Arapahoe Indians gave early Denverites. They said, *Heetno'-unoo'oo koh'oown*, or "The creek will flood." The predicted scenario occurred in 1863, with a devastating flood. Four floods later, in 1907, Denver Mayor Robert Speer began channeling Cherry Creek and landscaping its banks, creating a parkway that became Speer Blvd. Today, a 7-mile bike and pedestrian pathway follows Cherry

Creek from Confluence Park to the suburb of Cherry Creek. It's a long, bracing walk for the ambitious.

➤Walk on the pathway to a bridge over the creek just before the Champa Street overpass. Cross the creek and follow a long ramp up the west side of the Cherry Creek viaduct to the west side of Speer Blvd.

➤Walk along Speer Blvd. for a half-block to Arapahoe Street. Turn right onto Arapahoe. Cross Speer at the crosswalk to the southwest corner of the Denver Performing Arts Complex. Follow the stairways back into the Galleria and end the walk where you started at the intersection of Curtis and 14th streets.

Walk **5**

South Platte River Greenway

General location: A paved walk along the South Platte River greenbelt just west of downtown Denver.

Special attractions: South Platte River Greenway, Forney Transportation Museum, Confluence Park, Centennial Park, Gates-Crescent Park, Children's Museum of Denver, Platte Valley Trolley, and Colorado's Ocean Journey.

Difficulty rating: Easy. Following flat sidewalks, the walk is barrier-free and suitable for small children.

Distance: 2 miles.

Estimated time: 1.5 hours.

Services: Restrooms, picnic tables, and shelters along the trail.

Restrictions: Watch for bicyclists and rollerbladers. Leash your dog and pick up after it.

For more information: Denver Parks and Recreation Department, South Platte River Greenway Foundation.

Getting started: This walk begins from a large parking lot on the south side of Water Street immediately south of the Speer Boulevard bridge. The parking area is not accessible from Speer. To reach the lot from the south, take Interstate 25 to 23rd Avenue (Exit 211), or drive east on West 23rd Avenue from Federal Boulevard. From the north and downtown Denver, turn south onto Platte Street from 15th Street and drive past the Forney Transportation Museum to Water Street and the parking lot.

Public transportation: RTD buses serve the area. Check with RTD for routes and schedules.

Overview: This loop trail follows a short section of the South Platte River Greenway, a 10.5-mile route that parallels the South Platte River. Arising on the Continental Divide near Hoosier Pass, the South Platte runs 360 miles through Colorado and drains 28,584 square miles as one of Colorado's five major rivers. Its snowmelt-fed waters fuel the growth of Denver and its surrounding suburbs, then continue downstream to water the fertile fields and pastures along its broad valley in northeastern Colorado.

The South Platte has been abused, dammed, and diverted over time. In 1972, after the passage of the federal Clean Water Act, it was listed as one of the most polluted and endangered rivers in the nation. Abandoned warehouses and rusted industrial equipment lined the river, while untreated wastewater and chemicals were dumped into its once-clear waters. Environmental groups and civic appointees worked to rescue the waterway. In 1976, the nonprofit South Platte

South Platte River Greenway

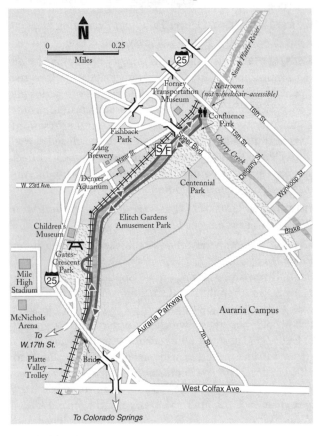

River Greenway Foundation was established to rehabilitate and coordinate the river's restoration.

Since then, the South Platte's course through Denver has been revitalized. A 10.5-mile paved trail now runs along its banks between Denver's north and south city limits. Parks, picnic areas, restrooms, and shelters sit alongside the pathway. Many Denverites use this special trail, including walkers, bicyclists, rollerbladers, anglers, and birders. Wildlife has also returned, and you may see deer, beaver, ducks, geese, and pheasants along the river corridor.

The walk

➤Begin in the large parking lot on the south side of Water Street, immediately south of the Speer Boulevard bridge. The parking area is not accessible from Speer. Go left (northeast) from the lot. (You can also walk in the reverse direction.) Keep an eye out for bicyclists who are also using the trail.

➤Step onto the paved trail above the west bank of the South Platte River and walk northeast under Speer Blvd. A portable toilet is on the left by the bridge.

Next to the parking area and the trail is historic Fishback Landing, the site of Thomas Warren's 1859 South Platte ferry service. In Denver's early days, the South Platte River was generally much larger than it is today, with fewer water-diversion projects along its course. The ferry was a necessity for prospectors who wished to cross the river en route to the Central City gold fields. Warren operated his chartered ferry for a few months before selling it and starting a brickyard. The ferry cost $1 for a wagon and team and twenty-five cents for each pedestrian.

As you walk along the greenway, note the chainlink fencing around many of the trees on the riverbanks. Why are these young cottonwood trees in fences? The wire cages protect the saplings from the Platte's burgeoning and transient population of hungry beavers. Nature's dam-building engineers, beavers love to eat cottonwoods, aspens, and willows.

➤After passing under Speer Blvd., the trail reaches Confluence Park. The park is the centerpiece of the South Platte Greenway, set at the confluence of two of Colorado's most historic waterways—the South Platte and Cherry Creek. Native Americans had long camped under cottonwoods and willows on the riverbank here. Stephen Long's 1820 expedition to the Rocky Mountains rested here, too, before exploring the Front Range. Twenty-two years later, one of John C. Frémont's railroad expeditions camped at the confluence. It was here in the summer of 1858 that a party of Georgia prospectors led by William Greeneberry Russell camped, panned for placer gold, and laid out a village they called Auraria after their hometown. Their finds precipitated the great "Pikes Peak or Bust!" gold rush during the late 1850s.

Dedicated in 1975, Confluence Park was the seed that grew into the South Platte Greenway Foundation. It was here that the restoration and transformation of Denver's waterways began. The park is the showcase of the entire greenway, with bridges that span the river, a brick plaza offering places to sit and picnic, a grassy amphitheater for concerts and outdoor events, and a plunging whitewater kayak chute.

The Forney Transportation Museum, just west of the greenway in an imposing red brick building, houses a large collection of railroad cars and engines, antique autos, carriages, and steam engines. Some of the highlights include a No. 4005 "Big Boy" steam locomotive, Amelia Earhart's Kissel Kar, an original McCormick reaper, and a 1907 limousine. The museum is in the 1901 Denver Tramway Company Powerhouse, a huge coal-burning power plant that once generated electricity for city trolley lines.

➤The walk crosses a pedestrian/bicycle bridge opposite the museum. Before you cross, walk north to Shoemaker Plaza on the west bank of the river. Plaques here honor the Platte River Development Committee and Thomas Hornsby Ferril's poem "Two Rivers," commemorating the famed confluence. Famous lines from the poem read, "Two rivers that were here before there was /A city here still come together."

➤Walk across the bridge just above the kayak run to the east bank. Head left to benches at an overlook above the South Platte and Cherry Creek confluence. A paved trail continues east from here along Cherry Creek into downtown Denver.

The main paved trail heads south under Speer Blvd. to Centennial Park, one of six parks along a 1.5-mile river stretch that make up the Riverfront Park system and the former site of a car crusher plant. Summer and fall bring spectacular plantings of colorful native and ornamental flowers. A few picnic tables beckon for a quick lunch.

Just past the park is Elitch Gardens amusement park. This popular, longtime Denver attraction moved from its old digs in northwest Denver to this scenic site along the Platte in 1995. It offers thrill-seekers more than twenty-one rides, including a wooden roller coaster and a whitewater ride, along with an observation tower and famed flower beds. The park is open daily in summer and weekends in spring and fall.

➤Continue south to an overpass that is the northbound highway entrance ramp from Colfax Avenue to Interstate 25. Cross the river on a bridge under the overpass and turn

Cottonwood shades a walker on The South Platte River Greenway.

right (north) on a tar path on the opposite (west) bank of the river.

➤Walk north to Gates-Crescent Park, another of the Riverfront Parks. This lovely 13-acre park spreads along the west bank of the South Platte, across I-25 from Mile High Stadium, home of the Denver Broncos football club. The park, partially funded by the Gates Foundation, offers parking, a playground, picnic tables, grass, and shade trees.

Paralleling the excellent paved trail is the Platte Valley Trolley. An old-fashioned fun ride on Trolley 1977 runs from 15th Street and Confluence Park south to Decatur Street on the west side of the river. Stops along the way allow access to Mile High Stadium, McNichols Arena, the Forney Museum, and the Children's Museum. The trolley offers both a half-hour and a 1-hour tour. Pay your fare when you get on board.

The Children's Museum of Denver sits on the north side of Gates-Crescent Park. This fabulous museum offers lots of hands-on exhibits and interesting displays. It's open Tuesday through Sunday.

➤Cross the trolley tracks near the Children's Museum. The green park fills the land between the sidewalk and the museum. Benches here offer marvelous views of downtown Denver's dramatic skyline as well as the futuristic sculptural towers at Elitch Gardens. A portable toilet is located here as well.

➤Continue down the trail past a large construction site. In 1999, this will be Colorado's Ocean Journey, a world-class aquarium sprawling across 16 acres. This unique aquarium will feature five indoor exhibits—Colorado River Journey, Sea of Cortez, Indonesia Tropical River Journey, Depths of the Pacific, and Ocean Discovery Plaza, along with an outdoor display of the Continental Divide.

Beyond the aquarium is the last standing building of the Zang Brewing Company. The brewery, once the largest west of the Mississippi River, was founded in 1850 by John Goode. Philip Zang, a German immigrant, worked his way up to plant manager and purchased the brewery in 1871. After an 1875 fire, Zang rebuilt the brewery in ten brick buildings that eventually produced 125,000 kegs of beer annually. Zang's son Adolph took over the brewery but sold it in 1889. The company continued producing beer until Prohibition, when it went to the opposite extreme and became an ice cream factory then went bankrupt. The hotel for the original brewery is now Zang's Brewery pub, with an outdoor patio.

➤Continue down the sidewalk and back to Fishback Landing, the parking area, and the walk's end.

Walk 6
The Grand Tour

The five walks in downtown Denver can be combined for a 10-mile Grand Tour. This lengthy walk, passing historic buildings, museums, shopping districts, and points of interest, will take at least 4 to 5 hours from start to finish.

The walk

➤Begin at the Denver Metro Convention and Visitors Bureau on West Colfax Avenue and follow Walk 1 to Broadway.

➤Turn right (north) on Broadway and walk a couple of blocks to the 16th Street Mall.

➤Follow Walk 2 down 16th St. to the RTD Market Street Station.

The Grand Tour

Map labels: Welton St., Lincoln, War Memorial Park, Colorado State Capitol, Judicial Bldg., Historical Society, Denver Public Library, Civic Center Park, Glenarm Pl., Tremont Pl., Court, California St., Stout St., Curtis St., Arapahoe St., Lawrence St., Champa St., 16th St. Mall, 15th, 14th, S/F, U.S. Mint, City-County Bldg., Denver Art Museum, Blake, Market, 18th, Wazee, Larimer St., Market Station, Tabor Ctr., Skyline Park, Writer Square, 7th, 20th, Union Station, 16th, Wynkoop, Larimer Square, Denver Performing Arts Complex, Curigan Hall, Colorado Convention Center, Auraria PKWY, St. Cajetan's Center, Auraria Campus, Collax Ave., Confluence Park, Forney Transportation Museum, 9th St., Platte River Greenway, Elitch Gardens, Tivoli Student Union, 8th St., 7th St., 5th St., 13th Ave., Water St., S. Platte River, 25, Aquarium, Children's Museum

Scale: 0   0.25   0.5   Miles

N

➤Follow Walk 3 through Larimer Square and the Lower Downtown district and back to the Market Street Station.

➤Walk back up 16th Street to Curtis Street. Turn right on Curtis and walk two blocks to 14th Street. Cross 14th to the Denver Performing Arts Complex and the start of Walk 4.

➤Follow Walk 4 through the Auraria Campus to Speer Boulevard.

➤Cross Speer to the Cherry Creek Trail. Follow steps down the trail and go right (northwest) on the paved trail alongside Cherry Creek for a mile to Confluence Park.

➤Follow Walk 5 along the South Platte River and finish back at Confluence Park.

➤Retrace the trail along Cherry Creek to Larimer St. Leave the trail and aqueduct and follow Larimer to 16th St.

➤Go right (southeast) on 16th St. back to Broadway (or take the free shuttle bus).

➤At Broadway, go right (south) back to Civic Center Park and follow the last part of Walk 1 back to the Convention and Visitors Bureau.

Walk 7
City Park

General location: A walk through City Park between the Denver Museum of Natural History and the Denver Zoo.

Special attractions: Denver Museum of Natural History, Denver Zoo, Park Pavilion, outdoor sculptures, formal rose garden, flower beds, and fishing lake.

Difficulty rating: Easy. Most of the walk is level with occasional gentle grades. The walk is paved except for a short gravel section, and is otherwise barrier-free.

Distance: 1.5 miles.

Estimated time: 1.5 hours.

Services: Limited services include a cafeteria and restrooms in the museum and the zoo. Other restrooms are located in the park pavilion.

Restrictions: The short gravel section southwest of the Museum of Natural History is not wheelchair-accessible, though strollers are okay.

For more information: Denver Parks and Recreation Department.

Getting started: Begin from the main parking lot on the north entrance side of the Denver Museum of Natural History, 2001 Colorado Boulevard. City Park is bounded on the west by York Street, on the east by Colorado Blvd., on the north by 23rd Avenue, and on the south by 17th Avenue. It is two blocks north of Colfax Avenue and just over a mile from downtown.

Public transportation: City Park is served by regular RTD bus service from downtown and Colorado Blvd. Check with RTD for schedules and route information.

Overview: Parks were important to Denver's citizens from the city's very beginning. Denver's first "parks" were beer gardens with flower beds, shade trees, and, of course, beer. The first city parks were proposed by Mayor Joseph Bates in his 1872 inaugural speech. Newspaperman William Byers also promoted the idea in his *Rocky Mountain News*, saying the city would not be perfect until "a public park is provided, like Central Park on Manhattan Island." A bill in the state legislature in 1878 allowed Denver to purchase 1,280 acres of state land for parks.

City Park, one of these parcels, was initially developed by Mayor Richard Sopris with a plan by Henry Meryweather in 1882. Water from Smith's (City) Ditch, a South Platte diversion project, ensured a plentiful supply of precious liquid for the park's first lawns and seedling trees. The park was designed in an English pastoral tradition, with encircling belts of trees that disguise the park boundaries. Lakes

City Park

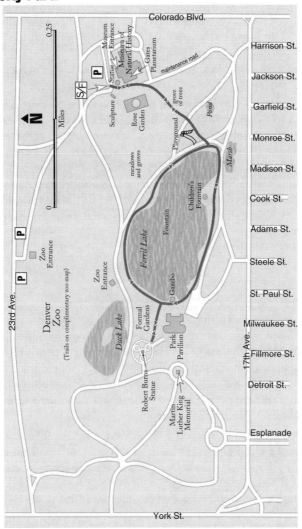

were laid out diagonally, and large meadows kept a feeling of open space. Meryweather's park plan allowed for foot and horse traffic and the installation of sculptures, gardens, and fountains. It was described as "pastoral, picturesque, naturalistic, and democratic."

Today City Park is still Denver's largest park. One mile long and three-quarters of a mile wide, it covers 317 acres. The lovely parkland encompasses two lakes, playgrounds, superb statuary, rose and flower gardens, picnic areas, several historic buildings, the 76-acre Denver Zoo, and the renowned Denver Museum of Natural History. Numerous paths and roadways thread among the park's woodlands and meadows, offering walkers a serene urban park experience. The described walk begins at the Natural History Museum and explores the Ferril Lake area via several paved and gravel trails.

The walk

➤ Begin from the Denver Museum of Natural History's parking area on the north (entrance) side of the museum. Follow a sidewalk around to the west side of the museum, past When Legends Run Free, a sculptural grouping of five bounding wolves, and The Grizzly's Last Stand, a bear statue donated to the park in 1930. The wolves, intentionally placed in a realistic setting among rocks and aspens, were sculptured by Rik Sargent in 1990.

➤ Follow the sidewalk left (southwest) to a terrace in front of the old museum entrance. The view west from here of City Park, downtown Denver, and the distant mountain skyline is one of Denver's best viewpoints. Sit on one of the nearby benches or sprawl on the grass and drink in the view for a few minutes before setting off on the walk.

of interest

The Denver Museum of Natural History

With its stunningly diverse displays, the Denver Museum of Natural History is one of the nation's best museums. It offers a spectacular dinosaur and fossil collection; displays of Native American culture; gems and minerals; an IMAX theater; the Gates Planetarium; and internationally recognized dioramas. The lifelike dioramas make us privileged viewers, able to peer through a tunnel of time and space to see animals in their native habitats and to experience the timeless magic of the natural world. One primeval scene includes a pack of Alaskan wolves poised on the frozen tundra, atop tufts of last summer's grass poking through fresh snow. In another, a herd of mule deer browse meadows below Pikes Peak on an autumn morning.

The dinosaur exhibit includes a 75-foot-long diplodocus, a 40-foot-long plesiosaur, and a stegosaurus, the Colorado state fossil. The mineral collection boasts "Tom's Baby," the largest gold nugget ever found in Colorado, and a king's ransom in other pieces of gold. The Crane American Indian Hall showcases collections from seven Native American cultural areas, including a Cheyenne village, Inuit kayaks and harpoons, Navajo weavings, and Hopi basketry and kachinas. The popular IMAX theater, with a screen three times normal size, shows numerous spectacular films that both thrill and amaze. The museum is open daily, except Christmas. An admission fee is charged.■

Just west of the sidewalk below the viewpoint is a reflecting pool and fountain surrounded by an immense formal rose garden. Stop by this exquisite garden on a summer day and smell the roses.

➤Walk south on the sidewalk to the southwest corner of the museum and locate a right-hand gravel path that threads southwest down a slight hill through a grove of towering spruce and pines along with catalpas and white oaks. A small rock amphitheater, the remains of a former watercourse, nestles among the trees below the path to the left.

➤The gravel path empties onto a closed road now used for park maintenance. Bear left toward a playground, which has portable toilets, benches, tables, and a drinking fountain. Keep left on a path around the left margin of the playground. If you have kids, they will not let you pass without stopping!

➤Continue along the pathway past a marshy pond edged with tall reeds, on the left. A few benches invite you to linger. Keep an eye out for magpies, abundant Canada geese, and the occasional kingfisher.

➤The path soon reaches Ferril Lake. This huge, glassy lake, formerly called City Park Lake, was renamed for Thomas Hornsby Ferril, Colorado's poet laureate from 1979 to 1996. A native Denverite, Ferril was born near here in 1896 and died at his Downing Street home in 1988. His home at 2123 Downing is now The Center for the Book. Ferril penned numerous poems about Denver and Colorado. His poem "This Lake is Mine" recalled his walking trips in City Park with his dog. The lake and adjoining Duck Lake, to the northwest, were built in the late 1880s and filled with water that ran from the South Platte River through the 30-mile-long Smith Ditch. The ditch, with more than 1,000 miles of lateral channels, brought lots of water into frontier Denver, allowing it to green and prosper.

➤The walk follows a paved trail along the south side of Ferril Lake. Its broad surface mirrors passing clouds and azure sky. Trees frame distant views of the downtown skyline and the mountains, including the rugged Indian Peaks

Skyline and Ferril Lake on the City Park Walk.

and flat-topped Longs Peak. Antique lightpoles topped with round glass globes line the lake trail. Occasional benches give you a chance to linger and gaze across the lake.

The sculptural Children's Fountain sits along the lake edge opposite a densely forested island. This white marble fountain, surrounded by an iron fence, features three nude children perched atop a streambank, exchanging glances with three bronze frogs. Benches allow contemplation. The sculpture, by French sculptor Max Blondt, was commissioned by Denver's famous mayor Robert Speer in 1912.

At the west end of Ferril Lake is City Park Pavilion, a large, tan, twin-towered stucco edifice built in 1896. It offers concessions (in summer) and restrooms. Immediately east of the pavilion, on the lakefront, is the 1896 Floating Bandstand, the setting for free concerts by the Denver Municipal Band over the last 100 years. New wrought iron fencing flanks the bandstand. Both the pavilion and bandstand were renovated in the 1990s as part of the City Park Pavilion Historic District.

A good side walk from the pavilion goes northwest 100 yards down a gravel path leading from the north side of the building into a beautiful formal garden filled with flowers and roses. Statuary, including a sculpture of a small child and a statue of poet Robert Burns, accents the gardens. The Burns statue was donated by the Scots Caledonian Club in 1904 in honor of the famed Scottish poet. West of the gardens is a massive 1976 statue memorializing Martin Luther King Jr. and the Civil Rights movement. Just north of the Burns statue is a park road and, beyond it, Duck Lake, summer home of a flock of black-crowned night herons. Beyond the lake lie the fenced confines of the Denver Zoo.

➤The walk continues from the pavilion along the concrete path on the north side of Ferril Lake, crossing a small bridge

of interest

The Denver Zoo

After your stroll through City Park, make sure you stop at the Denver Zoo on the park's north side. The zoo got its start with a bear cub named Bill Bryan in 1896. Today it houses more than 3,300 animals and more than 600 species from around the world. Representatives of almost 150 endangered species are found here, including three species already extinct in the wild. You may come face-to-face with elephants, rhinos, gorillas, polar bears, and king cobras. Of special interest is the Primate Panorama, home to twenty-eight primate species ranging from tiny pygmy marmoset to a 581-pound gorilla. The Tropical Discovery exhibit offers a stunning display of rain forest flora and fauna. The zoo is open year-round and charges a daily admission fee. Reach the zoo's southwest entrance by walking left (west) along the park road north of Ferril Lake. The main entrance is on the north side of the zoo on 23rd Ave., with a large parking area. Walking distance through the zoo is about 1.5 miles.■

then bending southwest. Flotillas of geese drift across the lake's smooth water, while an occasional cormorant, a seafaring bird, is seen drying its wings alongside the lake. The structural islands in the center of the lake are fountains, which operate in summer.

➤Continue around the lake until you reach a path that heads left past the north side of the playground on the lake's east side, then rejoins the first part of the walk at the closed maintenance road. Follow the gravel path northwest through trees to the Museum of Natural History.

Walk 8

Cheesman Park and Seventh Avenue

General location: A walk through the historic Seventh Avenue residential district and Cheesman Park in the Capitol Hill area, southeast of downtown Denver.

Special attractions: Denver Botanic Gardens, Cheesman Park, Morgan Addition Historic District, Seventh Avenue Historic District, Grant-Humphreys Mansion, and Quality Hill Historic District.

Difficulty rating: Easy. The walk is mostly level, on sidewalks. Lack of curb cuts on many corners makes the walk inaccessible to people in wheelchairs.

Distance: 3 miles.

Estimated time: 2 hours.

Services: Many services are found along the walk, including restaurants, a coffee shop, and a supermarket.

Restrictions: Dogs must be leashed in Cheesman Park.

For more information: Denver Parks and Recreation Department.

Getting started: The walk starts and ends at the large parking lot on the west side of Congress Park, which is on Josephine Street just north of East 8th Avenue. This lot is easily reached by driving south of York Street (one-way south) from Colfax to East 7th Avenue. Turn left on 7th and go east one block to Josephine Street (one-way north). The lot is one block north on the right.

Public transportation: Easiest public transportation to the walk's start is taking an RTD bus to the Denver Botanic Gardens. The walk begins just south of the gardens.

Overview: This walk traverses historic residential neighborhoods and Cheesman Park in the Capitol Hill area, southeast of downtown Denver. The walk goes past elegant mansions along relatively quiet city streets lined with tall, shady trees. Most of these residences were built by Denver's elite with money that came from burgeoning mining-related industries, transportation companies, and real estate transactions. Along with the mansions came schools and churches.

Originally dubbed Brown's Bluff, Capitol Hill surrounded the site of the proposed state capitol. The land was donated to Denver in 1868 by Henry Brown. From 1880 until 1910 many elaborate mansions were built along the hill's sandstone sidewalks, including the Governor's Mansion and the Grant-Humphreys Mansion. Much of the area's nineteenth-century architecture survived the demolition purge that decimated other parts of old Denver. Today the Capitol Hill area encompasses nine historic districts and numerous landmark buildings listed on state and national historic registers.

Cheesman Park and Seventh Avenue

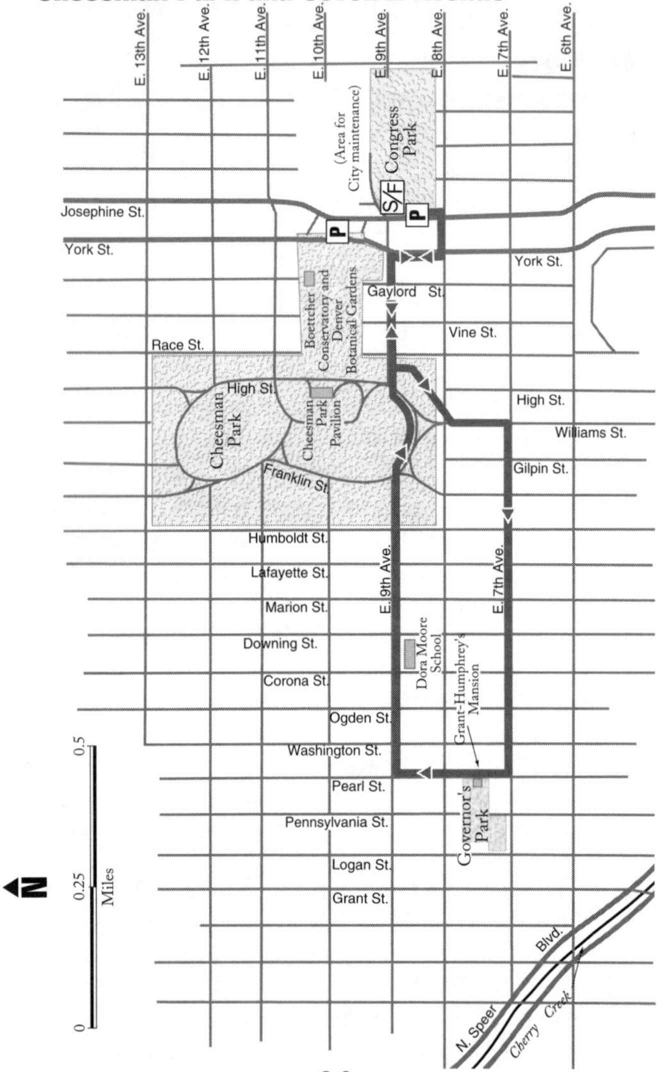

The walk

➤Start at the parking lot on the west side of Congress Park on Josephine Street and walk south to the corner of Josephine and East 8th Avenue.

➤Go west across Josephine at a crosswalk with a light and continue a block west to York Street. Cross the street at the crosswalk.

➤On the west side of York, turn right (north) and walk one block to East 9th Avenue and turn left (west). The walk heads west along East 9th for three blocks through the Morgan Addition Historic District. The subdivision was drawn up by Samuel Morgan and covered the south, Catholic side of the old city cemetery, which encompassed much of today's Cheesman Park. Between 1910 and 1930, after the cemetery was moved, its bones disinterred and reburied elsewhere, a selection of stunning and grand homes were built here. This historic residential district encompasses forty-five elegant homes, most designed in the Revival style.

➤When the sidewalk reaches the eastern edge of Cheesman Park, and 9th Ave. and merges with the park's roadways, turn left (south) on a park path that swings southwest through trees to 8th Ave. and a pedestrian/bike crosswalk with a signal light. Cross Eighth to a square block extension of the park called the Cheesman Esplanade, which connects the park with the East 7th Ave. Parkway.

➤Walk west a half-block along the north edge of the esplanade and 8th Ave. to Williams Street. Cross Williams and turn left (south). Follow the sidewalk south for one block to 7th Ave.

➤Turn right (west) on 7th and follow it for 1.2 miles to Pearl Street. This section of the walk traverses the heart of

of interest

Historic Homes

The Brown-Garrey-Congdon House, 1300 East Seventh, is a narrow, 100-foot-long townhouse that is only 18 feet wide. Built in 1921, the two-story stuccoed house is capped with a tiled roof. Miner Tom Congdon said living in the house was like "living on a bus."

The 1893 Mitchell-Schomp House at 680 Clarkson Street on the southeast corner of Clarkson and East Seventh, also called "Trail's End," was built in a Mediterranean style by John C. Mitchell, president of Denver National Bank. The eclectic two-and-a-half story and 13,000 square-foot house is surrounded by a wrought iron fence.

Farther west at 709 Clarkson St., on the northwest corner of the East Seventh–Clarkson intersection, is the brick Zang Mansion, a Capitol Hill landmark. This ornate Neoclassical Revival mansion was built by Adolph J. Zang for $108,000 in 1903. The mansion and its carriage house are now divided into offices. A two-story portico supported by balustraded Ionic columns frames the front door. Inside the house are hand-painted and gold-leafed ceilings, a Tiffany chandelier, five fireplaces, a third-floor ballroom, and ten varieties of wood used for paneling, doors, and carvings. Upstairs, a stained glass window features a colorful scene from Shakespeare's Merchant of Venice. Adolph Zang was the son of Philip Zang, the founder of Zang Brewery, the largest pre-Prohibition brewery in Colorado.

Another Mediterranean-style house is the Ferguson-Gano House at 722 East Seventh. This two-story "cottage" was the guesthouse for the now demolished Ferguson mansion.

The Wood-Morris-Bonfils House, at 707 Washington Street on the northwest corner of Washington and East

Seventh, is a beautiful Mediterranean-style residence originally built for Cripple Creek gold magnate Gulliford Wood.
It was later the home of *Denver Post* publisher Helen Bonfils
and now houses the Mexican Consulate.■

the East 7th Avenue Historic District, Denver's largest historic
district. Centered by East 7th Ave., the district is bordered
on the north by East 8th Ave. and on the south by East 6th
Ave. It includes 927 buildings that range from modest bungalows to elegant mansions.

Follow the sidewalks west along East 7th past a succes-
sion of lovely, well-landscaped houses. All of these homes
are evidence of care, pride, history, and taste. Many of
Denver's leading architects designed these residences in the
years after a trolley line enabled Denverites to move away
from the center of town into quieter suburban neighborhoods. Look for interesting architectural details, including
leaded glass, a variety of decorative brickwork, Greek-style
columns, porches, elevated entrances, stone and stucco pri-
vacy fences, and wrought iron gates and fences.

➤As you enter the Capitol Hill area, look for the intersection of East 7th Ave. and Pearl St. Cross Pearl and turn
right (north) on the sidewalk to follow its west side. Notice
the slabs of Lyons sandstone, quarried from the Front Range
northwest of Denver, which were used for sidewalk panels
and curbs. Much of the sandstone has eroded; it is being
gradually replaced with poured slabs of buff-colored concrete to match the original sandstone color.

The Grant-Humphreys Mansion sits on the west side of
Pearl between East 7th and East 8th avenues. This spectacular and beautiful mansion, now owned and operated as
a museum by the Colorado Historical Society, preserves a
slice of early Denver's history. Denver's most famous

Neoclassical landmark, the mansion was designed by architects Theodore Boal and Frederick Harnois for James B. Grant, a former Colorado governor and smelter tycoon. It was built between 1900 and 1902. After Grant's death in 1917, oil magnate Albert E. Humphreys bought the house and added a ten-car garage with gas pumps and a car wash for his fleet of Rolls Royces. His son Ira donated the mansion to the Colorado Historical Society to ensure that it would not be demolished for office space. The lavish residence features an immense semicircular portico supported by four fluted Corinthian columns. The building is characterized by its elaborate use of terra cotta, which replaced stone for ornament and trim at a fraction of the cost. Terra cotta became popular at the turn of the century as it offered more colors and better glazing than the previously used stone. The Grant-Humphreys Mansion used terra cotta on its window surrounds, porch balustrades, roof urns, and two-story columns. Plantings of oaks, firs, and spruces on the estate's grounds are well-tended, attaining very large proportions. Behind the mansion to the west is the grassy Governor's Park, with gardens, paths, and sculptures.

➤Walk north along Pearl St. and cross busy East 8th Ave. a half-block up from the Grant-Humphreys Mansion. On the southwest corner of Pearl and 8th is the John Porter House, a Tudor-style, red brick house that has been converted to offices.

As a side trip, walk two blocks west on East 8th to see the Governor's Mansion, home to Colorado's chief executive. This exquisite Georgian Revival mansion was built in 1908 for real estate tycoon Walter Cheesman.

➤On the main walk route, cross East 8th and walk north another block on Pearl until you reach East 9th Avenue. Turn right (east) on 9th.

Walker on Ninth Avenue.

9th Ave. is a very different street from elegant Seventh Ave. Instead of elaborate mansions and elegant homes, you'll find quiet neighborhoods with modest houses and newer condominiums and apartments. A four-block area north of Ninth between Logan and Clarkson streets is known as the Quality Hill Historic District. Quality Hill was called the city's "most exclusive residential section" by the *Denver Post* in 1901. Many of the area's mansions have been converted into apartment buildings.

►Continue east along East 9th. In a few blocks you will reach a small retail district with shops that cater to residents. Here is a King Soopers supermarket, Diedrich's Coffee (a good place to rest your feet and recharge yourself with their excellent coffee), a juice bar, a bagel bakery, and the Moore School.

On the south side of 9th, the Moore School was Denver's first school to be designated a historical landmark. The school board planned to tear it down, but the Denver Landmark Preservation Commission and the Denver City Council preserved it for its historical interest. The 1889 school was designed by famed Denver architect Robert Roeschlaub in a Romanesque Revival style with brick walls and terra cotta trim. Twin towers top its corners. Originally called Corona School, it was renamed in 1938 for longtime principal Dora Moore. It is still open as a school today.

►Continue east on 9th. The north side of the street offers sun on cool days, and the shady south side is ideal in summer. Walk east for three blocks, crossing the quiet streets of Downing, Marion, and Lafayette. Numerous apartment buildings with stylish architectural details flank the avenue. After three blocks you will reach Cheesman Park.

►Enter the park and walk east 100 feet to the main north-south trail on the west side of the park. Go right (south) on

of interest

The Ghosts of Cheesman Park

The old City Cemetery, Denver's first burying ground, was established a couple of miles east of central Denver in 1858 by William Larimer atop a 320-acre plot called Mount Prospect. This dry, rounded hillock offered marvelous views west toward the majestic, snowcapped Front Range. Over the ensuing decades, many of Denver's pioneer citizens, paupers, and desperadoes found their final resting places on this yucca and cacti-covered hillside. Since water was hard to come by, the cemetery (except for its Catholic and Jewish sectors) began to grow weedy and fall into disrepair. By the 1880s it was nicknamed Pauper's Hill because only the poorest were interred here. In 1887, one of the local newspapers wrote that it was "so ugly that if there are any buried there with any sense of the artistic or longings for the beautiful, they must turn over in their graves and groan at the thought of what is above them."

When the city fathers decided to turn the cemetery into Congress Park, they found no opposition. Beginning in 1888, graves were carefully disinterred by family members and organizations. Grand Old Army soldiers were reburied at Riverside Cemetery, while Odd Fellows and Masons relocated their loved ones elsewhere. The paupers were another matter, however. Undertaker E. P. McGovern was awarded a contract to remove up to ten thousand corpses from the cemetery. Each body was to be placed in a 12- by 42-inch box and reburied at another graveyard. The undertaker's crew soon began breaking up bodies and placing them in two boxes to reap extra profits from the dead. Graves were desecrated by this outrage, and also were plundered for jewelry and souvenirs.

Denver citizens were alarmed by this horror, but it was the dead themselves who seemed to rebel most against the disrespect. In the book *Twilight Dwellers of Colorado*, Mary Joy Martin notes: "In the darkness of night a constant moaning was heard upon the hill. Residents in nearby homes were disturbed by the sounds night after night. Low, almost melodious, the moaning was like the wind yet unlike the wind. There was a quality of deep sadness to it, and something hideous and chilling." Ghosts and shadowy figures were seen in houses and lurking in yards. Even today there are occasional hauntings here, the ghostly echo of a travesty that is long forgotten—except by those who still recline in silent graves under the green lawns at Cheesman Park. Old gravesites can be seen in the park on cold mornings, with their slightly sunken rectangles devoid of the night's frost.■

the asphalt trail. Cross 9th on the trail. Follow the trail around the south side of the park, to the right of Franklin Street.

Cheesman Park, originally named Congress Park in 1890, was renamed for real estate magnate Walter Scott Cheesman in 1907. It is one of Denver's original city parks. With its spacious grassy lawns edged by groves of trees, the park offers urbanites a green refuge. The centerpiece of the park is the Grecian-style Cheesman Memorial Pavilion. The 1910 memorial, finished three years after Cheesman's death, is a columned structure similar to the Parthenon in Athens, Greece. Reflecting pools and formal gardens that are bright with summer flowers surround the monument. The park itself is laced with curved pathways and roads.

➤Follow the path through the southern part of the park, slowly bending eastward along Franklin Street. Cross two park roads on pedestrian crosswalks, then bend northeast to East 9th Ave. Finish the walk by rejoining the 9th Ave. part of the walk. Follow 9th back to York Street. Go right (south) on York for one block to East 8th. Cross York at a crosswalk with the traffic light and continue east on 8th to Josephine St. Cross Josephine at a crosswalk with a traffic light and step left to your car in the parking lot on the west side of Congress Park.

Walk 9
Sloan Lake

General location: Sloan Lake Park in west Denver.

Special attractions: Sloan Lake, playground, boat ramp and rentals (summer), mountain views, and fishing.

Difficulty rating: Easy. Paved sidewalk all the way with wheel-chair curb cuts.

Distance: 2.3 miles.

Estimated time: 1.5 hours.

Services: Restrooms and a drinking fountain are found at the boathouse on the lake's north shore. Other restrooms are found at the playground off West 17th Avenue. Restaurants, a grocery store, and a convenience store are on Sheridan Boulevard, west of the park.

Restrictions: No swimming. Dogs must be leashed; pick up their deposits. Watch for bicyclists and rollerbladers.

For more information: Denver Parks and Recreation Department.

Getting started: The walk can begin at any of several parking areas on the perimeter of Sloan Lake. This description starts at the parking lot on the northwest corner of the park at the intersection of Sheridan Blvd. and West Byron Place. From downtown, go west on Colfax Avenue to Sheridan, turn right (north), and drive a few blocks to the park. Continue to the northwest corner parking lot.

Public transportation: RTD buses run from downtown to west Denver, passing Sloan Lake. Call for schedules.

Overview: Sloan Lake is the glassy centerpiece of Sloan Lake Park, a large preserve on the western edge of Denver. This land was once arid prairie, traversed only by a stagecoach and wagon track that connected Denver with the mountain gold fields. In 1861, however, farmer Thomas Sloan excavated a well and the next morning found a growing lake filling his property. It seems Sloan's well had penetrated a large underground aquifer that slowly drained onto the surface.

The 200-acre lake quickly became a popular summer recreation spot for Denverites, who rode out in carriages to enjoy swimming and boating excursions. *The City of Denver*, a small steam ship, cruised the lake's shallow waters from its berth at the nearby Grandview Hotel. Sloan's Lake Resort was opened on the lake's northwest shore by Adam Goff in 1890 and expanded by the Manhattan Beach Company in 1891 with an amusement park and sandy beach. The resort shut down after arson in 1908, was reborn as Luna Park, and closed for good in 1914.

By the 1930s, Denver had acquired the lake and the surrounding land, turning it into today's popular city park. Thomas Sloan left his lake in 1872, moving south to Pueblo, but his name remains on this lovely urban park and lake.

Sloan Lake

0.25

0 Miles

N

Mead St.

Newton

W. 20th St.

W. Lakeshore Dr.

Osceola

Perry

Cooper Lake

W. 22nd St.

W. 21st St.

Stuart Street

Park Road

Slight rise green hill

Island

Vrain St.

Utica

W. 17th Ave.

Vrain

Boat House year-round restrooms (not accessible)

seasonal restroom

Winona Ct.

W. Byron Place

Sloan Lake

Wolff St.

Boat Ramp

Bridge

S/F

lake inlet

Old Gun Club (closed)

Sheridan Blvd.

The walk

➤Begin from the spacious parking area at the northwest corner of the park off Sheridan Boulevard. The paved trail is obvious. The walk heads left (east) from here.

➤Walk past a boat ramp and follow the path along the north shore of Sloan Lake. The area to the north, now soccer fields, is the former site of Manhattan Beach. The 1890 Sloan's Lake Resort sat along the lake's northwest shore here and offered a pavilion for parties and concerts, along with boat rentals. Later, a small zoo, amusement park, and theater were added. Its beach was blanketed with imported California sand. No swimming is allowed in the lake today.

➤Curve north around the boathouse, a one-story building made of volcanic basalt. Restrooms, a drinking fountain, and a parking area are on the north side.

➤The trail continues along the north side of the old harbor, with boat docks to the south, before bending southeast. The Front Range, including 14,264-foot Mount Evans, often is reflected in the placid lake water. The long, tawny bulk of Green Mountain stretches below the higher peaks.

In late autumn and winter, keep an eye out along this stretch for large flocks of migrating waterfowl. Birds seen here include hundreds of Canada geese, mallard ducks, grebes, and seagulls.

➤The trail passes a couple of parking areas before it bends eastward. An offshore island separates Sloan Lake from Cooper Lake, which fills its eastern bay. Here the good concrete path ends and the trail is covered with older asphalt. Walk along the north shore and slowly trend around the east side of Cooper Lake. The elegant Tudor-style building that looms on the hill to the east is Lake Junior High School, built in 1926.

Walkers on the eastern shore of Sloan Lake.

➤The walk bends onto the south shore of the lake and heads west past a parking area off West 17th Avenue. Densely growing cattails line the lakeshore. Contorted, picturesque willows frame the shimmering lake and distant mountain views.

➤Keep on the paved path when it jogs south and crosses a park entrance loop road that leads to a couple of parking areas. Continue west under ponderosa pines, passing a fun playground and picnic tables with grills. The restroom here is open in warmer months, as are wheelchair-accessible portable toilets. South across 17th Ave. is St. Anthony's Hospital, founded in 1892 and now one of Colorado's largest hospitals.

➤Cross the park exit road and head northwest on a good concrete path around the southwest edge of the lake. A parking area and basketball courts are on the left. In the southwest corner of the park is the Submariner's Memorial, dedicated to the U.S.S. *Grayling*, which was sunk near the Philippines in 1943. The trail crosses an inlet creek on an arching bridge.

➤Walk north along the west shore of Sloan Lake and finish at the starting parking lot at the park's northwest corner. This final section of the walk offers great views of downtown Denver's skyscrapers, punctuating the eastern skyline.

Walk 10

Washington Park

General location: Washington Park, southeast of downtown Denver.

Special attractions: Smith Lake, Lake Grasmere, Smith's Ditch Historic District, formal gardens, fishing, playground, jogging, rollerblading, and bicycling.

Difficulty rating: Easy. The route is flat, on closed asphalt roads and sidewalks. The walk is barrier-free and good for small children.

Distance: 2 miles.

Estimated time: 1.5 hours.

Services: Restrooms and drinking fountains are found near the parking area, and there are portable toilets along the pathways. Other services, including restaurants and food, are available at shops on Alameda Avenue just north of the park.

Restrictions: Dogs must be leashed. Also, pick up after your dog. Watch for bicyclists and rollerbladers to avoid collisions.

For more information: Denver Parks and Recreation Department.

Getting started: Washington Park is easily reached from both downtown Denver and Interstate 25. Downing Street, a major north-south thoroughfare, borders the park on its west side. From I-25, take the Downing Street exit just west of University Street and drive north a couple of blocks to the park. Continue north another 0.5 mile and turn right into the parking area beside Smith Lake. The walk description begins and ends at this parking area. The trails are also accessed from many points around Washington Park.

Public transportation: The Washington Park area is served by RTD bus service from downtown Denver. Check with RTD for schedule and route information.

Overview: This walk follows paved trails and closed roadways through a long, narrow park located a few miles southeast of downtown Denver. The 162-acre park, offering welcome green space, sits in an old residential neighborhood. A couple of lakes—Smith Lake on the north side of the park and Grasmere Lake on the south—anchor respective ends. All roads through the park are closed to vehicular traffic, except for a short access road to a large parking area at Smith Lake. The roads are open to walkers, joggers, bicyclists, and rollerbladers. Several closed roads and trails lace the park, offering excellent walks that range from 1 to 2.5 miles. The described walk follows the main road/path through the park. You may want to explore more of the park on other trails.

Washington Park

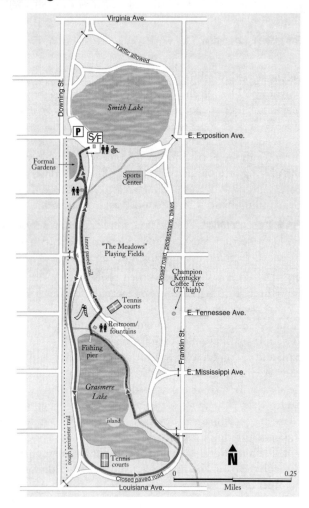

The walk

➤Begin from the parking lot on the southwest side of Smith Lake just east of Downing Street. Walk south from the parking area along a closed road that is divided into separate lanes for pedestrians and bikers. Keep a sharp eye out for bicyclists and rollerbladers while walking on the path. They can come up quickly from behind and startle you.

Immediately to the right is a large formal flower garden, courtesy of the Denver Parks and Recreation Department. It spreads a carpet of glorious and exquisite color here from May through October. You may want to explore the several paths that wind through the flower beds. At the north end of the gardens is a kiosk with plant identifications for each bed. Some of the flowers seen include coleus, zinnia, verbena, snapdragon, begonia, petunia, and geranium.

➤To continue the walk, return to the main road. The path is shaded by immense old cottonwoods, a common prairie tree that creates a shelter from wind and sun. A gravel path leaves from here and skirts the western perimeter of the park, rejoining the walk at the park's southwest corner.

On your right, on the west side of Downing, is a row of attractive, distinctive bungalows. Two of them are crowned with unusual roofs, with rounded lines reminiscent of thatched English cottages.

➤Just south of the gardens, you cross Smith's Ditch. This quiet waterway, lined with grassy banks, was Denver's first major irrigation ditch. Water diverted from the South Platte River allowed the area's dry hills and plains to blossom with grasses, gardens, and trees. Named for its engineer and financier John W. Smith, the 27-mile channel was dug by shovel and horse-pulled scrapers beginning in 1860. The ditch began at Waterton Canyon at the mouth of the South Platte's canyon in the lower Front Range. It traversed under today's Chatfield Reservoir, then flowed north through Englewood to the Capitol Hill area. Canals branched off from the main ditch, allowing water to feed other developments. After spending $10,000 to construct the ditch, Smith sold it to Denver in 1875 for $60,000. It was later extended to City Park and its water filled Ferril Lake. The ditch is now buried under Denver development, except for this last remaining section in Washington Park.

➤Continue south on the shaded road. Along the left (east) side of the road is the Great Meadow, a huge, level expanse of grass fringed by groves of trees. The meadow is divided into soccer fields for youth and adult leagues.

➤Keep right at a Y-junction just before the tennis courts. The closed-road path then edges along the western shore of Grasmere Lake. This large lake, shaped like a cowboy boot, is popular with anglers. A concrete-stepped shoreline retards erosion along the lake's strand. It makes a great spot to sit at the water's edge. Watch flocks of Canada geese drifting across the mirrored water or bask in the brilliant sunshine and watch the sun glint off wavelets. Benches are also scattered along the lakeshore and its various paths.

You will find a drinking fountain at the broad south end of Grasmere Lake behind more tennis courts. South High School sits across Louisiana Avenue from this end of Washington Park. During school lunch periods you may find yourself amid a group of teenage students relaxing in the shade of a cottonwood.

Other park trees include a deep grove of Douglas-firs south of the tennis courts. They are easily identified by their scaly cones and soft needles. Notice what appear to be tiny mice with protruding tails hidden within the cones' scales. Also present, American linden or basswood trees have broad

Formal flower beds in Washington Park.

leaves and long seedpods attached to a slender, leaflike scale. These occupy the grove alongside two venerable narrow-leaf cottonwoods that look suspiciously like weeping willows at first glance. Near the south end of the park along the park perimeter trail on the west side of Smith's Ditch paralleling Downing Street, are a couple of large Kentucky coffee trees. A 71-foot "Colorado Champion" Kentucky coffee tree is on the east side of the park.

From its earliest beginnings, Denver gave its open space parklands special attention. Using New York's Central Park as a model, the city contrasted open grass meadows with groves of trees. The groves are filled with either a variety of trees or a grouping of similar species.

➤The road bends along the southeast tip of the lake's boot, then turns north and away from its eastern shore. Step left on a short gravel path to the lake edge and follow a paved shoreline trail between the lake and Smith's Ditch. Continue walking along the lake to its northern end.

of interest

Historic Buildings

If you crave more walking, take the paved path around Smith Lake, the northern lake in Washington Park. This lake is also popular with anglers, who sit in lawnchairs on its shore and stick their poles in the sand as they wait for strikes.

Several historic buildings are located on the south shore of Smith Lake. The Washington Park Bathhouse was built in 1912 when the lake was a popular swimming hole. In 1996, the structure was renovated and is now the headquarters for Volunteers for Outdoor Colorado, a conservation organization. The Eugene Field Cottage, a rare 1880s wood-frame cottage, was moved here in 1927 to avoid its imminent destruction. It once was the home of Eugene Field, a noted journalist and poet who wrote the children's poem "Wynken, Blynken, and Nod." The cottage is on the east side of the park on the southwest corner of East Exposition Avenue.■

➤Rounding the northern shore of Grasmere Lake, notice the extended fishing pier that juts into the green lake water. Grasmere Lake is regularly stocked with trout by the Colorado Division of Wildlife for your angling pleasure. You will need a Colorado fishing license, available at any area sporting goods store. Do not pass up the chance to stroll onto the pier, with or without a fishing pole! It's a peaceful spot to watch trout leap for a passing fly or to listen for the chatter of the occasional kingfisher as it swoops above the water's surface. Linger awhile on the limbs of a twisted narrow-leaf cottonwood that hangs over the water.

➤From the lake's north end, turn right (north) and continue the walk by crossing a small bridge over Smith's Ditch to a short path that leads to a closed road on the right (east) side of the tennis courts. A playground on the right is an attractive stopover for those with frisky young children. A drinking fountain and portable toilet are also located here.

➤Complete the loop walk by following the road north to the Y-junction above the tennis courts. Rejoin the first part of the walk here and walk north to the parking lot at Smith Lake.

Walk 11

University of Denver

General location: The University of Denver campus in south Denver.

Special attractions: Observatory Park, Chamberlain Observatory, Professor's Row, University Hall, Iliff School of Theology Building, Evans Memorial Chapel, and historic homes.

Difficulty rating: Easy. The route is on sidewalks with curb cuts, accessible to people in wheelchairs.

Distance: 1.5 miles.

Estimated time: 1 hour.

Services: Restrooms are in Observatory Park north of Warren Avenue. Look for restaurants and service stations on Evans Avenue near the university.

Restrictions: Leash and pick up after your dog.

University of Denver

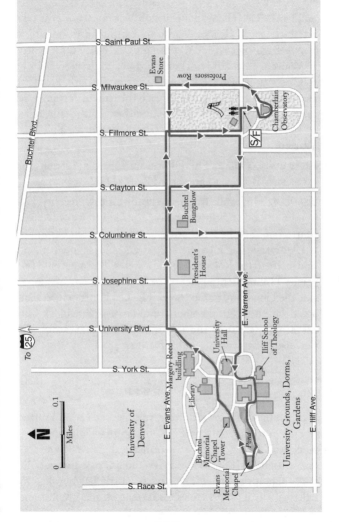

For more information: Denver Metro Convention and Visitors Bureau.

Getting started: The walk begins on Warren Avenue at Observatory Park. Reach Warren by exiting Interstate 25 at University Boulevard. Go south on University three blocks to Warren. Turn left (east) on Warren and drive five blocks to Observatory Park. Park on Warren at the park. From the east and Colorado Boulevard, reach the park by turning west on Evans Avenue and driving to either South Milwaukee or Fillmore streets. Turn right (south) and drive a block to Warren.

Public transportation: The DU campus, Evans Avenue, and University Boulevard are served by RTD buses.

Overview: This walk traverses the historic University Hill neighborhood and the campus of the University of Denver. Started in 1864 by Methodists as the Colorado Seminary, the University is both the largest and oldest independent university in the Rocky Mountain states. The adjacent University Hill residential area arose as a "college town" alongside the University in the 1880s. The neighborhood remains an enclave of historic homes around two-square block Observatory Park and the Chamberlain Observatory, the university's astronomical observatory.

The walk

➤Begin by walking south from your parked car on Warren Avenue into the main part of Observatory Park. The two-block park was laid out with symmetrical pathways and formal gardens in 1886. Warren Ave. did not pass through the park then; it does now. The park is mostly lawn broken by tall trees, including maples and ashes. A playground and

restrooms sit on the south end of the upper park sectio.
north of Warren.

➤Step around to the south side of the cut-stone Chamberlain Observatory, on the north side of the park. This celestial observatory, designed by famed Denver architect Robert S. Roeschlaub, opened in 1890. Roeschlaub also designed the nearby University Hall, as well as Trinity Methodist Church and the Central City Opera House. The observatory was built for wealthy amateur astronomer H. B. Chamberlain, who donated the building to the University of Denver. Considered one of the best nineteenth-century buildings in Denver, the structure is crowned by a gleaming iron dome that opens to allow an inside telescope to peer at the night sky. Nearby, to the southwest, is the smaller Students' Observatory.

➤Walk around the east side of the observatory back to Warren, then walk east on Warren to South Milwaukee Street. Cross at the intersection to the east side of the 2100 block of South Milwaukee and walk north on the sandstone slab sidewalk.

This block of lovely turn-of-the-century homes is called Professor's Row because professors at nearby DU lived here. Most of these homes were built between 1887 and 1898. Gray Gables (2184 South Milwaukee) is a Queen Anne-style house that was built for Episcopal Bishop Henry W. Warren and his wife Elizabeth, the widow of cattleman John W. Iliff. Note the spacious wraparound porch, the sandstone hitching post by the street, and the rear carriage house. Other houses of interest are at 2168, 2142, and 2118 South Milwaukee. The house at 2118 is different from the others with its Swiss influence. Look at its gables, large porch, and second floor brackets. The Kimball House, 2112 South Milwaukee, was the home of George Kimball, who owned the Kimball Red Sandstone Company, the main supplier of University Park's sandstone sidewalks. This house is a combination of Federal and Italianate elements, with iron cresting atop the roof and intricate brickwork.

➤At the corner of Milwaukee and Evans Avenue, turn left (west) and cross Milwaukee to the north side of Observatory Park. On the opposite (northeast) corner of Milwaukee and Evans is the old Evans Store, an 1888 brick grocery store built by ex-governor John Evans. The University Park Market was open until 1968. It is now office space.

➤Walk west along Evans Avenue to South Fillmore Street. Cross from the park to the west side of Fillmore and turn left (south) on Fillmore.

➤Follow Fillmore south to Warren Ave., passing more old homes. Of interest are numbers 2111 and 2127. The three-floor house at 2111 Fillmore has intricate shingling, detailed brickwork on the chimney, and an old stable in the rear. The Honeymoon Cottage, 2127 Fillmore, was often rented by newlywed university professors. The small cottage has leaded glass windows and courses of elaborate brickwork, including several button-shaped bricks.

➤At the corner of Fillmore and Warren, turn right (west) onto Warren. Walk west a block to South Clayton Street and turn right (north). More old and interesting homes are found on this block. Note the 1902 Shattuck House (2181 South Clayton), the classic Victorian cottage at 2140 South Clayton, and the Cutler House (2122 South Clayton). The 1890 Cutler House was the longtime residence of DU science professor Ira Cutler. The many tree species that Dr. Cutler planted in the University park neighborhood and on the DU Campus are part of his local legacy.

The Mary Reed Building, on the DU Campus.

➤At the corner of South Clayton and Evans, turn left (west) onto Evans and follow its south side to South Columbine Street. On the corner at 2100 South Columbine is the historic Buchtel Bungalow. This large bungalow built in 1905 was the residence of Methodist minister Henry A. Buchtel while he was Colorado's governor (1906–1908). Built in the popular turn-of-the-century bungalow style, the house has a homey symmetry with wide gabled eaves supported by large wooden brackets.

The house next door features a hand-carved wooden sculpture of a mountain lion and an eagle. The sculpture was hewn from the trunk of a dead, curbside silver maple tree by Arvada sculptor David Leon Mitchell in 1994. The rest of the block is lined with some of the neighborhood's best-looking houses, most of which were erected in Colonial, Victorian, and classic Edwardian styles.

➤Turn left (south) on South Columbine and walk one block to Warren. This block offers some of the neighborhood's finest houses.

➤At the corner of South Columbine and Warren, turn right (west) onto Warren Avenue. Walk two blocks west to South University Boulevard, passing more houses, student apartment buildings, and the University Park United Methodist Church.

➤Cross South University, a busy north-south street, at a crosswalk and stoplight. Enter the University of Denver campus.

➤Follow the sidewalk up University 100 feet and bend left along a cul-de-sac. The cul-de-sac is flanked by three massive buildings that dominate the DU campus. On the right (north) is University Hall; on the left (south) is the Iliff School of Theology Building; and straight ahead (west) is the large brick Mary Reed Building, dominated by its central brick tower.

University Hall, designed in the Richardson Romanesque style by Chamberlain Observatory architect Robert Roeschlaub, is a castlelike edifice built of cut stone in 1890. Now home to university offices, the hall once hosted many school functions within its classrooms and basement gymnasium.

Directly south of University Hall is the lovely Iliff School of Theology Building. This Denver landmark, built in 1892, presents an elegant Gothic facade on its north front. Note the building's gray granite foundation, red sandstone walls, and Gothic arch looming over the front doors and granite steps. The Iliff School of Theology was founded in 1892 as part of DU by Bishop Henry White Warren and cattleman John Wesley Iliff's family. In 1904 it separated from the University and now offers various religious programs and master's degrees.

►Walk west to the Mary Reed Building. After skirting it via a sidewalk along its south walls, walk down steps behind the building to the Mary Reece Harper Humanities Garden; wheelchair-accessible ramps are nearby. The garden has quiet pools studded with granite boulders. Its dense trees include junipers and blue spruces, with nearby benches for contemplation.

►Walk west through the garden to the Evans Memorial Chapel, a small stone church that was moved to the DU campus from its original site at West 13th Avenue and Bannock Street in 1960. The chapel's stones were carefully numbered before it was disassembled, then reassembled at its current site. This beautiful little chapel originally was built in 1874 for $13,000 by Governor John Evans as a memorial to his daughter Josephine. Note the pale Morrison sandstone walls, the Gothic arches, the iron cresting along the roof ridge, and the stone cross above the east gable. It is usually open during the day. Step inside the door on the south side for a glimpse of its stained glass windows.

➤Walk around the west side of the chapel on a sidewalk and keep right. Follow the sidewalk as it curves northeast and climbs a slight hill. Continue to a quadrangle and the modern Penrose Library, with a monolithic steel sculpture out front.

A bit farther on the sidewalk, on the left, is the Buchtel Memorial Chapel Tower, an Italianate brick tower that is the only surviving remnant of a chapel that was built here in 1907, completed in 1917, and burned in 1983.

➤Continue on the sidewalk past the large brick Margery Reed Hall and keep angling northeast to the corner of Evans Ave. and South University Boulevard. Cross University and head east on the south sidewalk of Evans. A large, green house along the way is the President's House (2100 South Josephine). This 1897 house on the southeast corner of Josephine and Evans was once the home for the Iliff School's president.

➤When you reach South Fillmore St. at Observatory Park, turn right (south) and walk one block to Warren Ave. and your car.

Walk 12
Crown Hill Park

General location: On the border of the suburban communities of Lakewood and Wheat Ridge, just west of Denver.

Special attractions: Crown Hill Lake, fitness trail, wildlife sanctuary, fishing, walking, and jogging.

Difficulty rating: Easy. The walk follows flat sidewalks and a good gravel trail. The paved/concrete section is wheelchair-accessible. The whole walk is suitable for small children.

Distance: 1.9 miles total, including the paved 1.2-mile Lake Loop Trail and the 0.7-mile wildlife sanctuary trail.

Estimated time: 1 hour.

Services: Restrooms, drinking fountains, and picnic facilities in the park.

Restrictions: The Kestrel Pond wildlife refuge is regulated to protect nesting birds. It is closed to all visitation from March 1

123

Crown Hill Park

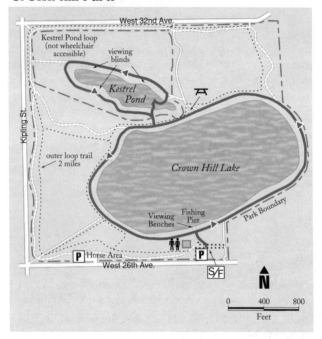

until June 30. In all parts of the park, hikers and joggers need to stay on trails and yield to equestrians. Keep an eye out for bicyclists and rollerbladers. All vehicles are confined to existing roadways. Dogs must be leashed in the park; they're not allowed in the wildlife area. Do not disturb any plants or animals. Watch for rattlesnakes in the grass along the trail.

For more information: Jefferson County Open Space.

Getting started: The walk begins at the parking area on the south side of Crown Hill Lake on West 26th Avenue. Reach West 26th and the park by driving north on Kipling Street from U.S. Highway 6 (Sixth Avenue) and West Colfax Avenue, or by going south on Kipling from Interstate 70.

Public transportation: The park area is accessed by RTD buses. Contact RTD for schedules and routes.

Overview: On the border of Lakewood and Wheat Ridge in Jefferson County, Crown Hill Park spreads across a low rise

of interest

Pond and Prairie

Crown Hill Park was established as a Jefferson County parkland in 1979, thanks to farsighted concerned citizens who saw a pressing need to preserve its pond and prairie in a natural state. The grassland area around Crown Hill Lake was designated open space, with reeds, cattails, and cottonwoods left to flourish on their own. In addition, a smaller area around Kestrel Pond in the park's northwest corner was protected as a wildlife sanctuary. This special resource area was dedicated as a National Urban Wildlife Refuge on Earth Day in 1991.

From the park's beginning days, only minimal public facilities have been constructed; the cost has been shared by the adjoining cities of Wheat Ridge, Lakewood, and Jefferson County. More than 300,000 people visit the park annually, livening its trails. Along with walkers, joggers, and rollerbladers, the park hosts optimistic anglers, their lawn chairs aligned for the best mountain views.

The natural qualities of this small parkland jewel refresh walkers, giving them a calm respite from Metro Denver's hurried daily schedules. It is comforting to know that this little treasure of prairie and pond ecology still exists. Its resident coyote family, magpies, ducks, geese, and snapping turtles can transport you into a quiet stillness that absorbs the traffic noise just beyond the park boundary.■

that offers splendid views of the Front Range, stretching from 14,264-foot Mount Evans to flat-topped, 14,256-foot Longs Peak on the northwest horizon. Covering more than 200 acres, the park is a wild enclave of open space. Expansive Crown Hill Lake, the surrounding grasslands, and the park's wildlife sanctuary are refuges for birds and animals in the midst of relatively dense suburban development.

This lovely 1.9-mile walk follows a paved trail around the lake before venturing into the wildlife area on a boardwalk and gravel path. It finishes by rejoining the paved lake trail. The walk yields great views of the snowy Rockies and allows you to experience nature in the city. As you walk through the wildlife refuge, pay attention to its diverse sounds—the muffled wingbeats of feeding ducks, the wind rustling through dry cottonwood leaves, the drums and horns of a marching band at nearby Wheat Ridge High School, and the distant murmur of traffic on city streets.

The walk

➤Park in the paved lot near the center of the park, accessed via West 26th Avenue. Restrooms, drinking fountains, picnic tables, and a park map are available here. To begin the walk, follow a concrete pathway that leads north toward Crown Hill Lake and the Lake Loop Trail.

➤At the lake, pause for a moment and enjoy a breathtaking view to the northwest past the tilted sandstone Flatirons above Boulder to distant, flat-topped Longs Peak in Rocky Mountain National Park. A couple of benches and a "viewing stand" are placed here so that gawkers can take in the scenic vista.

➤Go right (northeast) on the paved/concrete Lake Loop Trail, a 1.2-mile loop that forms a large oval around Crown

Hill Lake. Walking the trail in this direction gives you the best mountain views. Watch for speeding bicyclists and rollerbladers on the path. Although they are not supposed to speed, a few of them are maniacs. A park ranger regularly patrols the trail to keep speeding to a minimum.

There are numerous fishing spots along the shoreline. Regular local anglers have claimed certain areas for their own fishing pleasure. Opposite the parking area is a fishing pier for wheelchair-accessible fishing. The Colorado Division of Wildlife enforces all state fishing regulations here. All anglers must have a valid Colorado license.

➤The trail slowly curves around the east end of Crown Hill Lake. The shore is lined with densely packed cattails and reeds, with occasional tall cottonwoods. Due east of the lake and the park rises a sentinel tower that overlooks Crown Hill Cemetery. The land between the trail and the cemetery on the southeast side of the lake is the newest addition to Crown Hill Park.

Next, the path overlooks wild meadows filled with short grasses and sprinkled with wildflowers, including white prickly poppies in summer and blue asters in autumn. A few cottonwoods are taking root in the meadows. These water opportunists are the guardians of rivers and streams on the broad, arid Great Plains. Watch for poisonous hemlock, with carrotlike leaves and large umbrels atop sturdy stems. A form of hemlock was used by Greek philosopher Socrates to commit suicide. Cattails abound along the lakeshore, their elongated leaves offering perfect shelter for red-winged blackbirds.

Look for the swooping flight of a kingfisher as it searches for a fish meal. Flotillas of Canada geese, gulls, and ducks bob on the lake's wavelets. Lakeshore signs admonish, "Do Not Feed the Wildlife." Respect this warning. Birds and animals need to forage for their own food; human fare doesn't offer them a proper diet. They will not remain elegant, wild creatures if we make them dependent on handouts.

➤As the trail arcs around the north side of the lake, another pathway, the Outer Loop Trail, splits off to the right and follows the edge of the park along the bordering streets for 2 miles.

➤Continue walking along the lake to a ramada shading a picnic table. This shady structure makes a good resting point on hot days.

➤Continue on the Lake Loop Trail to a side path and a sign that points you north toward the Kestrel Pond wildlife refuge. Turn right here and follow a good gravel path that heads into a marshland on the southeast edge of the pond. An urban wildlife area, the marsh is fenced to keep pets out. Close the gate after you enter the area. Remember that the refuge is closed to all visitation from March 1 until June 30. At other times, walkers are allowed inside, but you must stay on designated paths to avoid disturbing plants, birds, and animals. The area is often patrolled by a park ranger to ensure that this rule is respected.

➤Close the gate behind you and walk to a floating plastic boardwalk that threads through the marsh. The boardwalk offers a rare view of a specialized plant and animal habitat. Tall cattails hem in the trail. Peek into the wavering rushes for glimpses of birds and water snakes.

➤After winding through the marsh you will reach another trail junction, on the marsh's north side. To your right is a gate and the picnic ramada. Turn left at the junction and walk northwest along the cottonwood-lined shore of Kestrel Pond.

Viewing blinds and benches along the pond's edge allow you to catch a glimpse of feeding ducks or perhaps a great blue heron wading in the shallow water. If you are walking here at dawn or dusk, be alert for the coyote family that lives in this remote part of the refuge. The coyotes are usually busy rearing pups. Their scat, or droppings, are often seen on the gravel trail. The coyotes have their own special human guardian, a Native American woman who regularly visits the park and serenades them with songs and chants.

➤At the west end of the pond, the trail bends sharply southeast and continues along the water's edge. Alongside the trail are huge bouquets of rabbitbrush, which explode with brilliant yellow flowers atop gray-green stems in late summer. Nettles and thistles grow in the dry grasslands beyond the trees, in sharp contrast to the lush lakeside ecosystem.

➤After circumnavigating Kestrel Pond, the gravel path returns to the gated entrance. Exit south through the gate, closing it securely.

➤Rejoin the paved Lake Loop Trail and continue southwest along Crown Hill Lake. In autumn, watch for snapping turtles crossing the trail as they migrate from the big lake to Kestrel Pond. At the west end of the lake, a couple of trails branch west to the Outer Loop Trail. These paths can be used to make longer loops for runners, horses, and walkers.

➤The paved/concrete trail continues around the southwest corner of the lake, with occasional scenic viewpoints along the lake's edge. It passes a few fitness stations then quietly ends at the grassy park north of the parking area. Step right to the restrooms, drinking fountains, shaded picnic tables, and your car.

Walk 13

Bear Creek Greenbelt

General location: A natural park along Bear Creek in Lakewood, southwest of Denver.

Special attractions: Open space, Bear Creek, the Stone House, ponds, birding, wildlife observation (bring binoculars), fishing, and bicycling.

Difficulty rating: Easy. Half of this level walk follows a paved trail; the other half follows gravel paths. The first half is wheelchair-accessible.

Distance: 2 miles.

Estimated time: 1 hour.

Services: Drinking fountain and restrooms at the Stone House parking area; no services on the trail.

Restrictions: Dogs must be leashed; pick up their deposits.

Watch for bicycles and rollerbladers. The gravel trail may be muddy in wet or snowy weather.

For more information: Lakewood Department of Parks and Recreation.

Getting started: The walk begins at the Stone House at 2800 South Estes Street. Get there by driving west from Interstate 25 or east from Colorado Highway 470 on West Hampden Avenue. Exit the highway onto South Wadsworth Boulevard and drive north to West Yale Avenue. Go left (west) on Yale and drive to South Estes St. Turn left (south) on Estes and park at the Stone House.

Public transportation: South Wadsworth Blvd. is served by RTD buses. Check with RTD for schedules and routes.

Overview: This walk explores a broad swath of undisturbed open space in the broad Bear Creek valley southwest of Denver. A couple of miles of creek and surrounding woodlands and prairie are protected as Lakewood's Bear Creek Greenbelt. This natural urban parkland is traversed by a concrete trail that begins at Kipling Street and runs east alongside Bear Creek all the way to the South Platte River Greenway (see Walk 5). This loop walk, following both concrete and gravel trails, samples the best parts of this urban corridor. It runs across broad grasslands, through groves of towering cottonwoods, and past prairie dog towns and placid ponds. Surrounded by busy streets and housing subdivisions, the quiet park is a place to get away from the city's bustle.

The walk

►Begin at the parking lot on the west side of the Stone House, on the east side of South Estes Street. A barrier-free, portable toilet is next to the lot.

Bear Creek Greenbelt

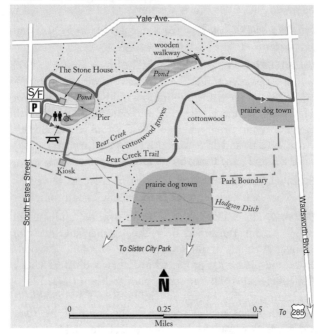

The Stone House, listed on the National Register of Historic Places, is a small cottage with sandstone block lintels and walls of fist-sized cobbles pulled from nearby Bear Creek's streambed. One of the few historic buildings left in southwest Denver, the house originally served as a stagecoach stop for passengers en route to the central Colorado mining town of Fairplay.

➤Walk right (south) from the parking area on a trail that leads southeast to a bridge crossing Bear Creek. The creek begins at melting snowfields that trickle into Summit Lake

132

below the snowcapped summit of 14,264-foot Mount Evans, 30 miles west of Denver. Emptying from the lake, the creek gathers tributaries and rushes down to Evergreen, where a dam stills its mountain waters. Bear Creek then tumbles through a sharp, ragged canyon near Morrison before emerging into a broad valley that runs through Lakewood and Denver to the South Platte River. The creek runs dangerously high in spring and early summer. Do not wade in it, and keep a watchful eye on small children.

➤Walk across on the bridge to a concrete trail on the creek's south side. A trailside kiosk here features a map of the Bear Creek Greenbelt. Turn left (east) on the concrete trail and walk 0.9 mile to South Wadsworth Boulevard. The popular trail threads among immense cottonwood trees and broad grassy meadows. Note the huge cottonwood where the path makes a sharp bend.

The cottonwood is a tree of the Great Plains. Out beyond the 100th Meridian, where most eastern tree species die from thirst and wind, the cottonwood comes into its own. Breaking the sweep of sky and grass, a giant cottonwood signified shade, firewood, and water for early pioneers. Cottonwoods thrive on floodplains like those along Bear Creek, rising to heights of 100 feet with trunks as thick as 7 feet.

Other natural features along this paved trail section are two prairie dog towns. One lies south of the trail at the base of a hill topped with rows of condominiums; the other is at the eastern end of the path, just before Wadsworth Blvd. Prairie dogs are common rodents in eastern Colorado, inhabiting grasslands and overgrazed pastures. These social animals live in underground towns. Look for them standing beside their burrows, with a lone sentinel watching for predators such as coyotes or hawks. Bring binoculars for a closer look.

A cottonwood tree towers above Bear Creek Greenbelt Walk.

➤Just past the second large prairie dog town, look for a short, rough gravel path that climbs to South Wadsworth Blvd. Exit the concrete trail here and walk up to the sidewalk on the west side of Wadsworth. The paved creekside trail continues east 4.3 miles to the Platte River Trail.

➤Cross Bear Creek on the street bridge to a trail that heads west from the north side of the bridge. Take the first gravel trail on the left, which dips and heads west along the creek's north bank.

The next 1.1 miles of the walk follow gravel trails across the open space north of Bear Creek. Lush vegetation lines the riparian zone, including willows and tall cottonwoods. Riparian zones are the most species-rich life zones in Colorado, with thick plant growth offering food and shelter to numerous bird and animal species. Beaver, mule deer, raccoons, and skunks live here. Look for birds in the trees. Hawks often perch atop the cottonwoods here, keeping sharp eyes out for rabbits, squirrels, snakes, and the occasional golden eagle.

➤At an oval-shaped pond, turn right onto another gravel trail. This path crosses an elevated boardwalk through a marsh. In season, red-winged blackbirds perch atop swaying cattails here. Beyond the marsh, the trail traverses open grassland before swinging back and rejoining the main trail at the west end of the pond.

➤Go right (west) on the main gravel trail for the last walk segment. The trail crosses more grassland, studded by cottonwoods, to reach another, larger pond. Follow the pond's north bank, then bend around its west end to finish at the parking area near the Stone House.

Walk 14
Belmar Park

General location: A quiet natural park in south Lakewood.

Special attractions: Lakewood Heritage Center, Kountze Lake, Weir Gulch, waterfowl, nature study, and historic buildings and artifacts.

Difficulty rating: Easy. With gentle hills and grades, the route follows concrete and packed gravel trails. The walk is barrier-free, but people in wheelchairs may want to stick to the paved paths.

Distance: 1.5 miles.

Estimated time: 1 hour.

Services: Restrooms and drinking water are found at the Lakewood Heritage Center at the beginning of the walk. Carry water in summer.

Restrictions: Leash your dogs and pick up their deposits. Watch for bicyclists and rollerbladers.

For more information: Lakewood Department of Parks and Recreation.

Getting started: Belmar Park and the Lakewood Heritage Center are at 797 South Wadsworth Boulevard. To get there from the north, drive south on Wadsworth from either Interstate 70 or U.S. Highway 6 (6th Avenue) to Ohio Street, just south of Alameda Avenue. Turn west on Ohio and drive one block. Turn left, following signs into a large parking lot. From the south, drive north on Wadsworth from either Colorado Highway 470 or Hampden Avenue to Ohio. Turn left (west) on Ohio and drive one block to a large parking lot on the left. The walk begins near the lot's southwest corner at the Heritage Center.

Public transportation: South Wadsworth Boulevard is served by regular RTD bus service.

Overview: This walk loops through Belmar Park, a 127-acre natural parkland administered by the Lakewood Department of Parks and Recreation. The park is a "passive system" with only native grasses, trees, and wildflowers which are left ungroomed and uncut. Its borders contain riparian, prairie grassland, and swamp ecosystems. A long concrete trail follows the park's perimeter, and the area is divided by intersecting gravel paths and horse trails.

The Lakewood Heritage Center occupies 15 acres of the park near its eastern boundary. The center, formerly the Belmar Museum, interprets Lakewood history with old houses and buildings plus a collection of antique farm machinery and implements. The center hosts community events, including Cider Days Harvest Festival, Old Glory Antique Fair, and the Mayor's Christmas Tree lighting ceremony.

Belmar Park

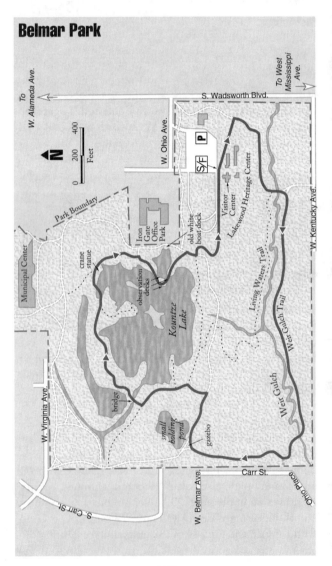

Belmar Park is part of the old May Bonfils–Stanton estate. The estate's mansion sat on the commanding hilltop just east of Kountze Lake. May Bonfils was the daughter of *Denver Post* publisher Frederick Bonfils. After his death, May inherited $10 million and used one million of it to erect her French-style mansion, complete with a lake and herd of tame deer. The estate was named "Belmar" by taking the first three letters of her mother's first name, Belle, and the first three letters from the Virgin Mary's name.

May bequeathed the mansion to the Catholic Church upon her death. The church was unable to fulfill the requests she made in her will, so the house was returned to her estate. Since May had stipulated that no one else could live in the house, her husband, Charles Stanton, had the mansion razed in 1970. Its only remains are the boat landing, a pumphouse, and the iron gates east of today's Irongate Office Park.

The walk

➤Beginning in the Lakewood Heritage Center, walk east from the visitor center down a road between old houses and sheds filled with farm machinery. Continue east past the buildings and angle right on a gravel path to a concrete trail.

➤Turn right (south) on the concrete trail and walk south down a slight hill parallel with Wadsworth Boulevard. Above the creek, step right on the trail and head west.

➤The walk follows Weir Gulch, a deep arroyo floored by a trickling creek at the bottom of a broad valley. This steep-walled gulch was carved by runoff from summer thunderstorms. Thick grass blankets the steep banks, and tall groups of cottonwoods scatter along the moist valley.

➤Keep left where the trail bends sharply to the left and crosses a bridge over the creek. Another path, the Living Waters Trail, begins here. This 0.9-mile trail threads through the south part of Belmar Park, passing a small creek that cascades through rock-rimmed pools below Kountze Lake.

➤Continue west above the south edge of the gulch. On the left, dry, grassy slopes rise to the park's southern boundary and West Kentucky Avenue. Near the west end of the park, the trail turns north and crosses the creek again on an elevated bridge.

➤Walk north on the concrete trail as it ascends a gentle hill studded with ponderosa pines. The trail divides after it reaches level ground. Take the right-hand fork at a gazebo next to a small holding pond. The left fork edges along Belmar Park's western and northern boundary before bending south along its east border.

➤Follow the trail for a couple hundred feet to another junction. Turn left (north) onto a gravel trail here. The walk follows the trail around the west and north sides of Kountze Lake.

The largest body of water in Belmar, Kountze Lake is home to many waterfowl, including Canada geese and a variety of ducks such as mallards and teal. If your eyes are sharp, you might spot a long-legged great blue heron feeding in the lake shallows or a red-tailed hawk perched atop a cottonwood limb.

➤Keep right at the first trail junction and walk across a plank bridge. A swamp rimmed by cottonwoods and cattails abuts the trail on the left. A bench here allows quiet reflection. Stop a moment and watch for red-winged blackbirds and feeding ducks.

Walking through Belmar Park.

➤Continue past the swamp and follow a boardwalk that spans an arm of the lake. On the shore just past the bridge is *Morning Mist*, a bronze statue of cranes by Greg Todd. The large, glass building to the north is the Lakewood Municipal Center, home of the suburb's municipal government.

➤The trail bends south from the statue to reach the east side of the lake. Follow the gravel trail until it intersects with the concrete loop trail. Keep right on the concrete trail.

A series of covered, wooden observation decks juts across the opening of a small bay. These decks offer a good resting place with benches, shade, and good views of swimming waterfowl. Look east across the lake from here to glimpse the white boat dock, one of the few remaining signs of the former Bonfils-Stanton estate.

➤Past the observation decks, the path joins the main concrete trail. Turn right and walk a short distance to a closed gravel road. Turn left onto the road/trail and follow it back to the Lakewood Heritage Center and the end of the walk. Before you leave the area, take time to explore the historical buildings and exhibits here. Restrooms, water, and a gift shop can be found in the visitor center.

Walk 15
Historic Golden

General location: West of Denver at the base of the mountains, in downtown Golden and on the Colorado School of Mines campus.

Special attractions: Golden DAR Pioneer Museum, American Alpine Club Museum and Library, Rocky Mountain Quilt Museum, Astor House Museum, The Armory Building, 12th Street Historic Residential District, Colorado School of Mines, National Earthquake and Information Center, School of Mines Geology Museum, Foothills Art Center, and Clear Creek Living History Park.

Difficulty rating: Moderate. The walk follows sidewalks except for a half-block section on Maple Street. Some hills.

Distance: 2 miles.

Estimated time: 1.5 hours.

Historic Golden

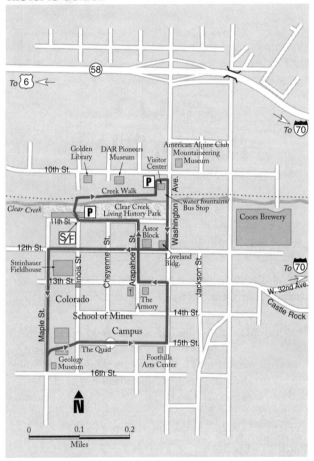

Services: All services along the walk.

Restrictions: The path is not wheelchair-accessible, but baby strollers are okay.

For more information: Golden Visitors Bureau.

Getting started: From Denver, follow U.S. Highway 6 (6th Avenue) or Colfax Avenue west to downtown Golden. Follow Washington Avenue, the main street through Golden, and turn west on 11th Street. Drive three blocks to several parking areas on the north side of 11th St. and park. The walk begins on 11th opposite its junction with Illinois Street.

Public transportation: Regional Transportation District (RTD) bus service runs to Golden from many areas of Denver including downtown, Denver International Airport, and Boulder. Call RTD for specific route information.

Overview: Nestled beside the banks of Clear Creek, below a mountain canyon, Golden is one of the oldest and most historic cities along the Front Range. To the east, two flat-topped mesas, North and South Table mountains, separate Golden from Denver's sprawling western suburbs, allowing it to retain its historic charm and small-town size.

The seat of Jefferson County, Golden was founded in June, 1859 as a supply center for miners bound for the rich gold fields around Central City. The town was named for local miner Tom Golden. It quickly became a transportation hub for freighters hauling goods to the burgeoning mining district. Golden was prominent enough to serve as territorial capital from 1862 to 1867. To get the appointment, its townsfolk offered a spacious meeting hall, free firewood, and $10-a-week rooms for legislators at the Astor House Hotel. Colorado's first railroad, the Colorado Central, came through town and up Clear Creek Canyon to

Central City in 1865. After the capital was moved to Denver in 1867, Golden continued to flourish as a supply town for miners and a transportation hub.

In 1874, Golden became the home of the Colorado School of Mines, now one of the nation's most prestigious mining colleges. The school had an unpaid faculty until the state began funding it in 1893. It was infamous for its wild male students, who frequently dropped out to go mining, and for its low graduation rate.

After the mining boom ended in the late nineteenth century, Golden assumed a quiet stability with an economy based on beer. Adolph Coors, a German immigrant, opened a brewery here in 1873. It has since become one of America's top five breweries in volume and Golden's leading employer and economic mainstay. Today Coors Brewery, using "Pure Rocky Mountain Spring Water," is considered the largest single-source brewery in the world, producing more than 20 million barrels annually.

Golden is one of Denver's most prosperous suburbs with its own thriving downtown area, the renowned School of Mines, and a burgeoning commuter population. Concerned citizens have saved most of Golden's historic buildings with the 1983 Historic Preservation Ordinance and a seven-citizen board that designates significant local landmarks and historic districts.

This walking tour explores much of Golden's colorful heritage. After the walk, experience some of Golden's other offerings by taking the free Coors Brewery tour, visiting the unique Colorado Railroad Museum, and driving up Lookout Mountain to Buffalo Bill Cody's gravesite.

The walk

►Begin at the free streetside parking area on the north side of 11th Street at its junction with Illinois Street. The parking area is in front of the Clear Creek Living History Park. Walk north and cross Clear Creek on a wide footbridge to the right (north) of the parking area. Once you are on the north bank, turn right on a gravel path that follows the creek eastward. This trail is the Creekwalk, which runs alongside Clear Creek from the Coors Brewery to a campground at the west end of 10th Street.

Clear Creek is one of the major streams in the Front Range west of Denver. It springs from melting snowfields atop the Continental Divide at Loveland Pass above Eisenhower Tunnel. The creek tumbles east through a glacial-carved valley to Georgetown and then Idaho Springs. Below Idaho Springs it rumbles through sharp Clear Creek Canyon, an abrupt gorge sliced into the ancient bedrock west of Golden. This rugged canyon, followed by U.S. Highway 6, is popular with gold panners, hikers, and rock climbers. In Golden, Clear Creek is a broad, rushing stream floored with worn cobbles and boulders. Use caution along its banks in spring and early summer when the creek is deep, frothy, and filled with winter snowmelt. Golden residents have long utilized the creek for water, irrigation, and industry, including sawmills, smelters, and, of course, its famed Coors beer.

The Golden Library, a branch of the Jefferson County library system, is just north of the walk at 1019 10th St. Organized in the early 1900s, the library moved to its current location in a former recreation center in 1996. It offers a large collection of Golden history documents, books, and newspapers, including microfiche copies of the *Golden Transcript* newspaper dating from its 1868 inception.

➤The walk continues along the creek to the Golden DAR Pioneer Museum at 923 10th St. Step around to the front of the museum to its entrance. This free museum yields a fascinating glimpse into Golden's long and colorful history as the territorial capital and gateway to Central City's gold fields. More than four thousand historic items, artifacts, and photographs trace the Golden area from its prehistoric days through the mid-twentieth century. Among the exhibits are a Native American doll collection, mining tools, pioneer clothing and implements, and the town's first galvanized bathtub. The museum is open daily except Sundays and holidays.

➤Continue east, passing benches that overlook the creek's torrent. Note the wire fencing that protects the base of small and medium-sized cottonwoods along the bank. Beavers have felled unprotected trees, one of their favorite foods, leaving only gnawed stumps on the stony banks.

➤Pass behind the brick Golden City Hall and Police Station to reach the Golden Visitor Center and Chamber of Commerce on the corner of 10th St. and Washington Avenue. The center offers information, maps, and brochures about Golden and the surrounding area. You can find restrooms here and a drinking fountain outside on the building's southeast corner. A major bus stop is located here on Washington Ave.

Across the street is Parfet Park, a grassy square shaded by huge cottonwood trees. A marker on a boulder here designates the place where George West built a log, two-story Boston Company store in 1859. In the old Golden High School, on the northeast corner of Washington and 10th, is the American Mountaineering Center. The center is the headquarters of the American Alpine Club and Colorado Mountain Club, and houses a mountaineering museum and one of the world's largest mountaineering libraries.

Looking down Washington Avenue, Golden.

➤Where the Creekwalk intersects Washington Ave., turn right and walk south along Washington on a wide bridge over Clear Creek. This is the latest in a series of bridges that have spanned the tumbling water. The first one here was a toll footbridge erected by John Ferrell in 1859; he later widened it for wagons and livestock.

➤Continue south from the bridge and enter Golden's charming downtown district centered on Washington Ave. This street has always been the town's commercial hub. It boasts a wide variety of architectural styles that date from the late 1800s to modern times. A 1992 revitalization project renovated Washington Ave., making it more pedestrian friendly. Sandstone benches, colorful flower plantings, and Victorian street lamps encourage walkers to linger.

The "Howdy Folks" Arch, spanning Washington between 11th and 12th streets, is Golden's most famous and noticeable landmark. The arch was built in 1949 for $7,500.

➤Walk south on the west side of Washington for one block. This single block is chock full of historic buildings. Across the street is the Rocky Mountain Quilt Museum (1111 Washington). Dedicated to the old American folk art of quilting, the museum features rotating displays from its large collection based on themes such as "Quilts Made by Men," "Then and Now" (old and contemporary versions of the same patterns), and "Houses in Quilts: The Fabrics of Our Lives." The museum also has a gift shop, educational programs, demonstrations, and lectures.

The two-story, brick Coors Building at 1120 Washington was built by Adolph Coors in 1906. It held a tavern that was owned by Charles Sitterle. The saloon featured Coors beer until it closed during Prohibition.

At the corner of Washington and 12th Street is the historic W. A. H. Loveland Building, an imposing brick building that once housed Colorado's territorial legislature. One of Colorado's most historic structures, the building was erected by W. A. H. Loveland in 1863. An early entrepreneur, Loveland was also a legislator, a railroad man with the Colorado Central Railway, and owner of the *Rocky Mountain News* and *Denver Post* newspapers. In sessions held here in 1866–1867, the territorial legislature took part in Golden's battle with neighboring Denver over which town would become the capital. The outcome was decided by a single vote in 1867, and the capital moved to Denver. Though it was rumored that the vote was bought, the charge was never validated.

From 1868 until 1941, Nicholas Koenig and his son operated the Koenig Grocery here, and from 1941 to 1971 it was the Golden Mercantile. Later it became the Mercantile Restaurant, which in 1997 became the Old Capitol Grill. The building was restored to its 1905 appearance in 1993.

►At the Loveland Building, turn right (west) on 12th St. Go past the building, crossing Miners Alley, and pass a public restroom made from quarried sandstone. You'll soon reach the Astor House Museum on the northeast corner of 12th and Arapahoe streets.

The Astor House (822 12th St.) is another one of Golden's historic architectural treasures. This 1867 three-story stone hotel is listed on the National Register of Historic Places. It was the first stone hotel built west of the Mississippi River, and is now the oldest hotel in Colorado. Seth Lake built the hotel, with its 18-inch-thick walls, in Frontier Georgian style. It was meant to accommodate territorial legislators, who met across the alley, charging $4.50 a week for room and board. By the time it was finished, however, the legislature had already bolted for Denver. In 1892, Ida Goetz bought the place for back taxes. Establishing a boarding house called the Boston House, Goetz catered to School of Mines students. In the early 1970s, the hotel was slated for demolition, but concerned Goldenites rallied and saved it. Now the white hotel is run as a museum that depicts Golden's history and exhibits a legislator's suite, a miner's room, and a kitchen with a wood stove and hand pump. It is open Tuesday through Saturday from 11 A.M. to 4 P.M. An admission is charged.

►Cross Arapahoe Street and continue into the 12th Street Historic Residential District. The walk heads west on 12th for three blocks to Maple Street.

The 12th Street Historic Residential District is a simple yet elegant neighborhood of narrow, tree-lined streets and graceful, unpretentious houses built in the late nineteenth century. Most of the homes are made from local clay bricks and have shingled roofs, wraparound porches, turrets, and bay windows. Look for circular Local Landmark plaques beside the front doors of historic houses. The first historic house is the Standley House (900 12th St.), a gabled brick dwelling built in 1873 for Joseph Standley. The Thomas Gow House (906 12th) is an 1879 cottage that was built for $700. The Kelly Mansion (920 12th) is a lovely two-story residence built in 1879 for Golden physician, territorial legislator, and mayor James Kelly. The house is an excellent example of the popular mid-nineteenth-century Italianate style. In the mansion's backyard, you'll find the Golden City Brewery. Inquire for tours and samples.

The next two blocks of 12th St. offer more historic homes. The charming Maddox Home at 1006 12th was built of brick in 1903 for $2,800. Other interesting residences are the 1897 Sorenson Home (1010 12th), the 1893 Parshall Home (1014 12th), and the 1872 West Home (1018 12th).

This lovely Gothic cottage was owned by George West, publisher of the *Golden Transcript*, the state's oldest weekly newspaper. Historic houses in the 1100 block include the 1874 Welch House; the 1873 Dennis House; the 1874 Whitehead House; the 1871 Titus House; and the 1876 Kimball House. This last house, on the corner, has curved window tops and a carriage house in back.

➤At the corner of 12th and Maple, turn left (south) on Maple and begin walking up a long hill. The second half of the block has no sidewalk, so walk along the curb as you head up Maple past a few homes.

➤Cross 13th Street to reach the Colorado School of Mines campus. The School of Mines has long been one of Golden's greatest assets. Golden was designated the site of the territory's mining school in 1870, beating out rivals Denver and Central City. The college worked with the mining industry, developing new smelting and assaying techniques. Today, with an enrollment of three thousand undergraduate and graduate students, the school is considered one of the nation's best mining, energy engineering, and geology colleges. The school's mascot is a prospector's burro, and its team moniker is the Orediggers.

On the southeast corner of Maple and 13th streets is the Steinhauer Field House, a beige brick building erected in 1937. Note the bas-relief sculpture of the burro, miner's pick, and shovel beside the arched window. Continue uphill on Maple past the Arthur Lakes Library to the backside of Guggenheim Hall. This administration building was built in 1905 with an $80,000 donation from Senator Simon Guggenheim of the famous Guggenheim family, which gained much of its fortunes from smelting. The three-story brick building is topped with a gold dome cupola above a bell tower.

➤Continue south to ornate Berthoud Hall on the corner of Maple and 16th streets. This hall, built in 1938 and trimmed with elaborate terra cotta details, houses the School of Mines Geology Museum. The entrance to the free museum is on Maple St. It keeps a veritable treasure trove of exquisite mineral specimens and gemstones from around the world. Exhibits trace the history of mining in Colorado with artifacts and ore samples. A collection of fossils depict life through the ages. The Museum is open daily (hours vary).

➤Continue the walk by stepping north to the north side of Berthoud Hall. Note the exquisite and ornate facade on the hall. Locate a tar path that heads east between Guggenheim and Berthoud halls and passes a sculpture of two burros by Robin Laws. The path meets the sidewalk in front of Guggenheim Hall at Illinois Street.

➤Cross Illinois St. at a pedestrian crosswalk to reach the left side of a grassy square called Kadafar Commons. Students sit under the shade trees here studying mineralogy or run on the grass playing football and frisbee.

A good sidewalk goes south along Illinois to the National Earthquake and Information Center (1711 Illinois). Run by the U.S. Geological Survey, the center monitors seismic activity around the world and investigates earthquake, geomagnetic, and landslide hazards. Tours and information are available.

➤Continue the walk by following the sidewalk along the north side of the grassy quad to a circular turnaround on 15th Street. The sidewalk goes east on 15th to Arapahoe. Cross Arapahoe and look north. The three-story red brick and stone building on the north side of the street is the 1894 Hall of Engineering, the oldest building on the campus.

►Walk down 15th St. to Washington Ave. On the southwest corner of the intersection is the historic First Presbyterian Church, now the Foothills Arts Center. The red brick building, with arched windows and doorways and a square bell tower, was constructed in 1872 on land donated by W. A. H. Loveland. Famed mountain circuit-riding preacher Sheldon Jackson served the church. When the congregation moved to a larger space in 1970, it sold the old church to local artists and art patrons who converted it into a regional art center. The Foothills Arts Center is Golden's leading bastion of culture, offering shows and exhibitions by local and regional artists. Step inside the center's six galleries for a look at the current exhibitions. Admission is free.

On the northwest corner of 15th and Washington is the historic 1879 Richard Broad House. This restored house, updated in the Queen Anne style at the turn of the century, is now the Antique Rose Bed and Breakfast Inn.

►Turn left (north) on Washington Ave. and follow a sidewalk down a steep hill into Golden's downtown area. Cross 14th Street to the pedestrian mall.

At 1310 Washington, the Table Mountain Inn is a longtime Golden lodging establishment. Redesigned in a Southwestern Pueblo Revival style with pink stucco exterior and tile roof in 1992, the inn was originally the Berrimoor Hotel and later the LaRay Hotel. Lu Holland renovated it in the 1940s as the Holland House.

►Continue north on Washington to the Bent Gate Climbing Shop on the corner of Washington and 13th Street. Turn left (west) on 13th. You'll pass a good bookstore en route to Arapahoe St. On the north side of 13th is local landmark Foss Drug, a huge drugstore that began in 1913 with the slogan "Where the West Shops." The south face of the drugstore building is graced with a mural by artist Robert Dafford which depicts Golden's early history.

On the corner of Arapahoe and 13th is the Armory, a massive cobblestone building looming above the sidewalk. Reputedly the largest cobblestone building in the United States, this structure was built in 1913 with 3,300 wagonloads of cobbles pulled from Clear Creek. Originally the headquarters for Colorado National Guard Company A, today the Armory houses offices, computers, and telephones instead of rifles and ammunition.

On the opposite corner is Calvary Episcopal Church, the state's oldest operating Episcopal church. The brick sanctuary was erected in 1867.

➤At the Armory, turn right (north) on Arapahoe St. and walk two blocks to 11th St., passing the Astor House along the way.

➤Cross 11th St. and turn left (west). Walk two blocks, passing the Clear Creek Ranch, a living history area that illustrates Golden's early years. On this strip of land above Clear Creek are a couple of log cabins, a schoolhouse, and a barn relocated here in the 1990s. Run by the Golden Landmarks Association, the site offers historic displays and activities in summer.

➤Finish the walk at the west end of the ranch, when you reach the parking area on 11th St.

Walk 16

Pearl Street Mall– Mapleton Hill

General location: In Boulder, northwest of Denver, along the Pearl Street pedestrian mall and in the historic Mapleton Hill area.

Special attractions: Pearl Street Mall, Squires-Tourtellote-Malick House Museum, Mapleton Hill homes, Hotel Boulderado, shopping, dining, and historic buildings.

Difficulty rating: Easy. The walk follows paved sidewalks with some gentle hills. The Pearl Street Mall section is barrier-free and suitable for people in wheelchairs.

Distance: 1.1 miles.

Estimated time: 1 hour.

Pearl Street Mall—Mapleton Hill

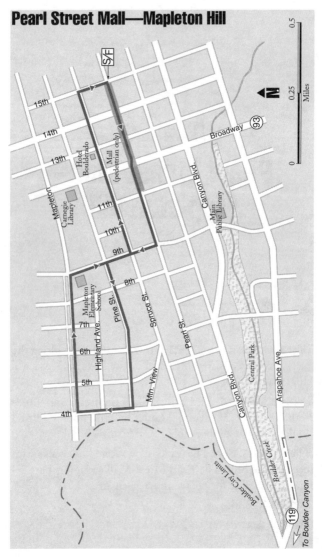

Services: All walker services are found on the mall, including restrooms, drinking fountains, restaurants, and shopping.

Restrictions: None. Keep your dog leashed and pick up its droppings.

For more information: Boulder Chamber of Commerce.

Getting started: The walk begins at the east end of the Pearl Street Mall in downtown Boulder at the junction of Pearl and 15th streets. From Denver, enter Boulder on U.S. Highway 36, which turns into 28th Street. Drive north on 28th past Arapahoe Boulevard and Canyon Road to Pearl St., just north of Crossroads Mall. Turn left (west) on Pearl and drive until it dead-ends at the pedestrian mall. Many parking lots and on-street metered parking spaces are found near the start of the walk.

Public transportation: Downtown Boulder is accessible via Regional Transportation District (RTD) buses from Denver. Check with RTD for schedules and routes.

Overview: Boulder is a small, cosmopolitan city that lies a scant 30 minutes or 27 miles northwest of Denver. Surrounded by open space, the compact community nestles in the broad valley of Boulder Creek below an abrupt mountain escarpment. The mountain front is protected as Boulder city parkland, and lifts immense Flatirons of sandstone high above the town. Boulder is home to the University of Colorado (CU). It boasts a diverse and eclectic population that places a premium on quality of life. Superb recreational opportunities include rock climbing, hiking, mountain biking, trail running, and walking.

In the early 1960s, proposed developments on the Front Range above Boulder awakened citizens to the need for open space, parks, and protected vistas. In 1967, Boulder became the nation's first city to tax itself for the acquisition of open space. Today, Boulder County boasts well over 32,000 acres of parkland, forming Colorado's largest urban park system. Miles of trails thread through Boulder County, exploring its mountains and pacing along its city streets. This walk introduces you to historic Boulder, following the famous Pearl Street walking mall before making a loop through the old residential Mapleton Hill district.

Pearl Street Mall won national acclaim after it opened in 1977. Boulder decided to turn one of its busiest downtown streets into a four-block-long pedestrian mall that is now the city's vibrant heart. The mall is a fabulous place to watch people. You can see every type of Boulderite here—students, shoppers, browsers, street musicians, jugglers, mimes, and business people. Numerous historic buildings are found along the mall. Fascinating shops include bookstores, a kite shop, jewelers, chic boutiques, specialty gift shops, and art galleries. Numerous restaurants line the mall. Look for the 14th Street Grill (outdoor patio dining), Pour la France, and the Falafel King, an inexpensive cafe with great Mediterranean cuisine. The Walnut Brewery and Oasis Brewery are both situated on the mall.

The walk

➤The walk begins at the east end of the Pearl Street Mall at the junction of Pearl and 15th streets. Walk west on the mall for four blocks to 11th Street. Pedestrian crosswalks with traffic lights are at all the street crossings. The mall is wheelchair-accessible, with curb cuts. Lots of benches allow for rest, relaxation, conversation, and people-watching. The first mall block offers lots of shops and a sculpture garden with a beaver, a snail, a rabbit, and a frog for kids to play on.

The city's historic County Building towers above the north side of Pearl Street between 13th and 14th streets. After the first county building burned down, this modern building was erected in 1933 using Dakota sandstone that had been quarried in 1882 near Fort Collins, Colorado. The stone came from bridge abutments on the abandoned narrow-gauge Switzerland Trail Railroad in the mountains and cost the City of Boulder a mere $25 plus the cost of hauling. A frieze depicts two of the county's former occupations: farmer and miner. The fountain in front of the building offers four drinking pools for passing dogs. On its southwest side, a statue memorializes Brigadier General Nathaniel Lyon, the first Union general killed in the Civil War. There are public restrooms in the building.

➤The Macky Building (1240 Pearl) is one of Boulder's oldest commercial buildings. It was built in 1860 by A. J. Macky, a New Yorker who moved west in 1860 with gold fever and became a successful Boulder businessman. The old Fonda Drug Store Building (1218 Pearl) was erected in 1893 for local druggist George Fonda, who was a volunteer fireman and played the tuba in the local band.

➤Cross Broadway. The intersection of Broadway and Pearl is Boulder's birthplace. It was here, in February 1859, that a group of fifty-four prospectors drove a stake into the ground and founded the Boulder City Town Company. A. A. Brookfield, one of the founders, wrote his wife, "We thought that as the weather would not permit us to mine, we would lay out and commence to build what may be an important town." The one-hundred lot town languished as a few log cabins scattered on the treeless hills near Boulder Creek until gold and silver was discovered west of here. Isabella Bird, an Englishwoman who traveled through the area, said Boulder was "a hideous collection of frame houses on the burning plain."

By the late 1800s, Pearl Street was the commercial center of a thriving Boulder, a distinction it again holds. Historic buildings in the 1100 block include the Voegtle Building on the northwest corner of Pearl and Broadway, the Boettcher Building at 1144 Pearl, the Boulder City Building at 1136 Pearl, and the Buckingham Building on the corner of Pearl and 11th streets. The 1911 Voegtle Building was a fruit market and later housed a clothier. The Boettcher Building was built in 1878 to house Charles Boettcher's hardware store. Boettcher went on to become a leading Colorado industrialist and philanthropist. The 1882 Boulder City Building, with its brick facade and elaborate cornices, was a hardware and mercantile store. The Buckingham Building was erected in 1898 to house the National State Bank. This bank, founded by Charles and Walter Buckingham in 1874, is the oldest operating business in Boulder.

➤The mall ends at 11th St. Continue west on Pearl St. to 9th Street. Historic buildings on this stretch include the 1899 McDonald Building (1039 Pearl), one of old Boulder's many saloons, and the Arnett Hotel (1025 Pearl).

➤Turn right (north) on 9th St. and walk up a slight uphill rise for two blocks to Pine Street.

➤Turn left (west) on Pine St. Here the walk enters the historic Mapleton Hill area, one of Boulder's oldest and most elegant residential neighborhoods. The Mapleton Hill Addition was platted by the Boulder Land and Improvement Company in 1888 on land purchased from the federal government by Frederick Squires and Jonathan Tourtellote. Back then it was a desolate, treeless, windswept ridge dotted with yuccas and protected by rattlesnakes. Jane Sewell, daughter of CU's first president, described her first view of this part

Walkers on the Pearl Street Mall, Boulder.

of Boulder: "No tree nor shrub nor any human habitation was in sight. Vast expanses of rock and sagebrush were its only surroundings." Today the hill is a lovely area to walk through, with prestigious homes and wide, quiet streets lined with white and sugar maples and oaks that were planted in the 1890s. Boulder is now a national "Tree City" with more than forty thousand trees along its streets and parks.

The Earhart-Degge House, on the northeast corner of Pine and 9th streets, was built in 1879 in the Federal style. A block up Pine on the northeast corner of Pine and 8th streets is the McKenzie House, a beautiful Victorian home built by banker and mining man Neil McKenzie in 1890. McKenzie made his fortunes from the Poorman silver mine in Caribou, west of Boulder. The clapboard house features a wraparound porch, elegant scrollwork, and a turreted loft. On the southwest corner of 8th and Pine is the Fonda House, the 1901 home of Pearl Street druggist George Fonda. He undoubtedly disturbed the McKenzies' evening peace with his tuba practice!

➤Continue west up Pine St. toward the mountains. Some of the older homes here are the 1895 Dodge House and the 1903 Lewis-Cobb House. The Dodge House, on the southwest corner of Pine and 6th streets, was the home of prominent local physician Horace O. Dodge.

➤At Fourth Street, turn right (north) and walk two blocks to Mapleton Avenue.

➤Turn right (east) on Mapleton. Walk almost 0.5 mile down Mapleton, a broad avenue with a maple-lined median, to 9th St. You will pass numerous elegant residences, including exquisite cut-stone homes in the 400 block. At the corner of Mapleton and 9th is the Mapleton Elementary School. This old school, built in 1888, is still in use.

➤Turn right (south) onto 9th Street. The sidewalk drops downhill past the school. Continue south across Highland and Pine streets to Spruce Street.

➤Turn left (east) on Spruce St., which parallels the Pearl Street Mall one block to the north. This street also preserves many historic homes.

At 1019 Spruce, the historic Squires-Tourtellote-Malick House is now operated as a unique museum by the Boulder Historical Society. Possibly the oldest house left from Boulder's raucous pioneer days, it was originally built in the 1860s by the Squires and Tourtellote families, who shared the house. The families (the wives were twin sisters) emigrated here from Illinois in 1860 and became prominent in town politics and at the University of Colorado. This is the only historic home in Boulder open to the public.

At 1105 Spruce is the 1894 Paddock Home, once the residence of prominent Colorado journalist Lucius Carver Paddock. Paddock started a weekly newspaper here in 1885 then purchased the *Boulder Daily Camera* in 1892. He served as its publisher and editor for forty-nine years. After he retired, his son Alva continued the tradition for another twenty-one years.

The Coates House (1123 Spruce) was built in 1872. This brick colonial home is now office space.

At the corner of Spruce and Broadway is the Willard Building. This 1898 edifice was built by Prohibitionists Albert Reed and Frederick White. It was named for Frances Willard, the president of the Women's Christian Temperance Union. Boulder became a "dry" town thirteen years before Prohibition and stayed dry for fifteen elections afterward.

➤Cross Broadway and continue east on Spruce St. The famed Hotel Boulderado sits on the northwest corner of

Spruce and 13th streets. This grand old hotel, its name a combination of Boulder and Colorado, was built in 1906. No two rooms are alike in the Victorian inn. The hotel was built after Boulder City Council members decided that the town needed a first-class hotel; they mounted a subscription campaign that raised the building funds at $100 a share. The hotel was publicly owned until 1940.

➤Cross 13th St. and continue east on Spruce to 14th St.

➤Cross 14th St. On the north side of Spruce between 14th and 15th streets are the First United Methodist Church of Boulder, built in 1891, and the Allen-Faus House, dating from 1874.

➤At 15th St., turn right (south) and walk one block to the eastern end of the Pearl Street Mall and your starting point.

Walk 17
Central City

General location: Historic Central City, an old gold mining town in the mountains west of Denver.

Special attractions: Central City Opera House, the Teller House, Central City National Historic District, Gilpin County Historical Society Museum, historic buildings and homes, casino gambling, and scenic views.

Difficulty rating: Moderate. Some hills and stairs.

Distance: 0.8 mile. A longer loop up to the town cemetery adds 2 miles to the total.

Estimated time: 1 hour.

Services: All services are found along the walk, including restaurants and restrooms in casinos.

Restrictions: You will have to climb hills and stairs, and Central City's high elevation may cause shortness of breath and

167

fatigue. There is really no free parking anywhere in the area; parking is not allowed on city streets without permits. Look for one of the many pay lots scattered around. Some of the biggest are just south of Main Street. Farther south, up the hill, is a public lot.

For more information: Check in on the ground floor at City Hall for visitor information and maps.

Getting started: Central City is 35 miles west of Denver in the mountains. The easiest and most scenic approach is via U.S. Highway 6 up Clear Creek Canyon from Golden. Follow US 6 to its junction with Colorado Highway 119. Turn right (north) on CO 119. Continue to Black Hawk. Turn left in Black Hawk and follow the road up the gulch to Central City. The walk starts at City Hall at the intersection of Main and Nevada streets on the south side of town. It's best to pay to park in a casino lot and take that lot's shuttle down to Main Street.

Public transportation: Central City is served by gambler buses from Denver. Check with the Denver Convention and Visitors Bureau for information.

Overview: This walk provides a glimpse into Central City's mining days, passing stately Victorian homes, old storefronts and elaborate facades pasted onto today's stores and casinos, and the tailings and crumbling headframes of old mines. The town has a lovely ambience, especially off-season when fewer tourists and gamblers walk its streets. In summer, come prepared for traffic congestion and parking problems. There is virtually no free parking in the area. The walk follows sidewalks and the sides of narrow roads; both are sometimes in disrepair. Central City sits at a lofty 8,560 feet above sea level, so take your time if you are unaccustomed to higher elevations.

Central City

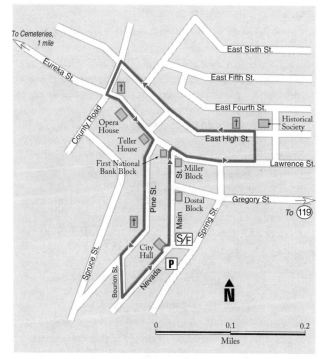

The walk

►Begin outside City Hall at the three-way intersection of Main, Spring, and Nevada streets on the south side of town. Step inside for visitor information and a town map. City Hall was built in 1897 as a residence. The two-story brick building's left side is original, while the right wing was added in 1992. It was briefly a casino before Central City established its city offices here in 1995.

of interest

Central City's Past

Denver and Central City are irrevocably entwined. Small placer deposits were initially found downstream in the gravels along the South Platte River and Cherry Creek at the site of today's Denver in 1858. The following year, John Gregory worked his way up Clear Creek, finding bits of color that convinced him that somewhere upstream was a rich lode. The trail of gold dust led him to a side gulch where he struck gold in a decomposing quartz vein on May 6, 1859. Gregory had stumbled onto treasure; he took out more gold in his first week than all of Cherry Creek had yielded in the previous year.

Word of the discovery spread like wildfire, and the "Pikes Peak or Bust!" gold rush was on. Within weeks of Gregory's strike, more than five thousand miners teemed into Gregory's Diggings to seek their fortunes. The rush emptied the towns of Denver and Auraria on the prairie below, involving many miners who had trekked across the plains only to be discouraged by the scant gold found at Cherry Creek. Horace Greeley, renowned editor of the *New York Tribune*, visited the Central City area to investigate the veracity of the gold stories. The miners welcomed him by "salting" a placer mine with a few shotgun blasts of gold dust. The next morning the boosters invited Greeley to pan some gold and he was amazed by the quantity. His glowing report of the Gregory Diggings intensified the gold rush.

Several camps sprang up on the steep mountain slopes, including Gregory Point, Black Hawk, Mountain City, Central City, and Nevadaville. Two of the camps prospered into burgeoning towns—Black Hawk, dubbed for the trademark of an early mining company, and Central City, named for the town's central location among all the camps. By the mid-1860s, Central City's population exceeded 15,000 and the rich town boasted a diverse, cultured, and cosmopolitan air. The townspeople enjoyed opera, theater, and musicals in the Montana and Belvidere theaters, and later in the ornate Central City Opera House. A Protestant church was organized here, and miner's courts kept law and order, which were sometimes quick and lethal. One local judge had his own "Local Uplift Society," which hanged eighty-eight men and seven women from the branch of a tall tree. The mining town's dark side is further revealed by a police report from an 1861 election, reporting "217 fistfights, 97 revolver fights, 11 Bowie knife fights, and 1 dog fight." Two fires, in 1873 and 1874, decimated much of Central City's business district.

Central City flourished on the riches that were extricated from the surrounding mountains and gulches. The Gregory Mining District, nicknamed "The Richest Square Mile on Earth," steadily produced riches for the remainder of the nineteenth century. Numerous prospectors found their mother lode and basked in wealth and power; others made fortunes in retailing and business. The new millionaires included future U.S. Senator Henry Teller and Jeremiah Lee, a 29-year-old ex-slave of Confederate General Robert E. Lee. Jeremiah Lee's OK Mine yielded the fabulously rich Argentine Lode. Teller, a local attorney, built the elegant Teller House hotel here in 1872. When President Ulysses S. Grant stayed there in 1873, he found the path from his carriage to the hotel paved with silver bars.

Central City's gold production peaked in 1878. After that, the mines' output slowly dwindled with the rise of the other Colorado silver towns such as Leadville in the 1880s and the gold camp of Cripple Creek in the 1890s. The area's fortunes sagged, and by 1900 the town settled into a quiet retirement. Almost all mining had ceased by 1930. Central City's second rush began with a whimper when the town's

Opera House was refurbished and reopened in 1932 with a lavish production starring Lillian Gish. Music lovers began coming to the quaint town nestled among scarred hills to hear their favorite operas and see the nation's best dramatic artists. Tourists also came to relive the colorful history of the first and best preserved of Colorado's mining camps.

Writer Jack Kerouac penned his 1950s Central City experience in his Beat Generation novel *On The Road*: "Central City is two miles high; at first you get drunk on the altitude, then you get tired, and there's a fever in your soul. We approached the lights around the opera house down the narrow dark street; then we took a sharp right and hit some old saloons with swinging doors." The town was designated a National Historic District in 1961, reflecting a strong preservationist ethic among its residents. The latest chapter in Central City's history came in 1991 with the legalization of limited-stakes gambling. Economic prosperity has again returned to the city, with casinos occupying the old buildings on Main Street.■

➤Walk north along Main Street into the heart of Central City. This narrow, two-block street is lined with charming Victorian buildings that are filled with history. Many now house casinos and gift shops. To appreciate the architectural details, admire the buildings from the opposite side of the street. Some of the buildings have historical plaques that detail their colorful stories.

Buildings of interest along the west side of the street are Armory Hall, the AOUW Building, the Meyer Building, the Roworth Block, the IOOF Building, the Elks Lodge, and the First National Bank Block. Buildings on the east side of the street are the Gold Coin Saloon, the Dostal Block, and the Miller Block.

Armory Hall was originally the Belvidere Theatre, a predecessor to the Central City Opera House. Central City's first theater opened in 1860, a year after the town's founding. The Montana Theatre opened in 1863 and ran shows until it burned down in 1873. In 1875, the Belvidere replaced the Montana, offering plays on its second floor while other businesses, including a grain company, bottling works, and fire department, used the first floor quarters.

The AOUW Building was built as a one-floor structure in 1874 and used as a clothing store and then the town post office. Its original cast iron storefront was installed in 1874. The Ancient Order of United Workmen, a fraternal organization, bought the place in 1897 and added the second floor for their meeting room. The post office occupied the ground floor until 1938. Because of its thick brick walls, the building survived the town's great fire of 1874.

Next door is the Meyer Building, another 1874 one-floor building with a second story added by Ignatz Meyer in 1901. It became Emily Wilson's famous Glory Hole Saloon in 1948, named for the rich Glory Hole Mine. Wilson acquired the solid walnut bar, which came from Missouri by ox cart, in 1859. The backbar came from the nearby ghost town of Baltimore. Today, the historic saloon is known as the Glory Hole Casino.

The Roworth Block, also known as the Sauer-McShane Mercantile, holds the oldest buildings on Main Street and the only ones to survive the devastating 1874 fire. The north building was built in 1863 as the Central City Bakery, and the south one was built in 1868 as a grocery store.

Across the street is the Gold Coin Saloon, which opened in 1897 and served as a bar except during Prohibition years, when it was a pool hall. It became a casino in the early 1990s. Note the building's facade, which is crooked along the top.

A mine tunnel under the building collapsed in 1900, shifting the foundation and causing the slant.

The IOOF Building, on the west side of the street, was built in 1874. The International Order of Odd Fellows, one of the city's twenty fraternal organizations, bought this hall in 1878 and used it as their lodge until it became a casino in 1991. Its facade features a cast iron front and an ornate pressed metal cornice with elaborate brackets and an ornamental sign on top.

On the east side of Main Street is the Dostal Block, one of the oldest and best preserved blocks of shops in town. This brick block, built in 1874 for $3,000, has decorative brickwork and a bracketed metal cornice on its facade. It initially housed a meat market, billiards hall, and the Empire Bakery.

►The block ends where Gregory Street meets Main. On the west side of Main Street is the three-story Elks Lodge, now housing a candy store and gift shop. The building was erected in 1874 after the catastrophic town fire. The Elks added the third floor and elaborate cornice in 1902.

Past the Bonanza Casino on the corner of Main and Eureka/Lawrence streets is the First National Bank Block. Founded in 1863, the bank moved into these quarters after the 1874 fire. Luckily, a fireproof vault had preserved all the bank's important papers. The spacious building, which wraps around the corner, has a brick facade, arched French windows, and a detailed cornice. The bank closed in 1933 and a casino now operates here. A flume carries Eureka Creek under the building and Lawrence St. becomes Eureka St. at its intersection with Main.

On the opposite corner of Main and Eureka is the Miller Block, another brick block erected after the 1874 fire. It was originally a grocery store, then the Chain O'Mines and Golden Rose hotels, and is now a casino.

Colorful storefronts along the Central City Walk.

➤Cross to the north side of Lawrence St. and turn right (east). Walk east past shops and decaying storefronts. Buildings of interest here are the 1874 Pharmacy, the oldest drug store in Colorado; the 1875 Wells Fargo Express Office with its cast iron front; the 1875 Mellor Block, which housed a bank, clothing shop, and grocery store; and the Edmundson Block, three brick buildings built as an investment by local physician William Edmundson. Past the Granite House, an old boarding house with stores on its lower level, is Raynold's Beehive.

An old and important Central City building, Raynold's Beehive was a large brick structure built in the 1860s to house the Hazard Powder Company. After the stout building withstood town fires in 1873 and 1874, it became "a beehive of activity" as the temporary quarters of numerous burned-down local businesses. One local wrote, "At one time after the fire, Raynolds' office and warehouse furnished accommodations for one bank, several mining companies, a meat market, a boot and shoe store, and a clothing store, while what space that was left went to the dogs and cats." Now it's busy as the Central Palace Casino.

➤Beyond Raynold's Beehive, turn left between buildings onto a ramp, then head up a long wooden staircase that climbs north to High Street. The building to the right of the stairway is an old school. At the top of the stairs is High Street, an east-west street perched above the town.

The large granite edifice on your right is the old Central City High School, now the Gilpin County Historical Museum. Walk up the sandstone stairs and sidewalk to the building. Along with the schoolhouse in Black Hawk, this was one of the first two permanent schools built in Colorado. This 1870 structure cost the lordly sum of $20,000, much of it due to the cost of freighting materials up here. The museum exhibits photographs, artifacts, and displays of Central City's colorful past. It's open daily Memorial Day through Labor Day. Admission is charged.

Next door to the museum is St. Paul's Episcopal Church, an elegant cut-stone church erected in 1874. The congregation was organized by Reverend Joseph Talbot in 1860 and worshipped in a wooden church on Lawrence St. until it burned in the 1873 fire. Church members then built this Gothic Revival church. Note the pointed window arches and the towering steeple.

➤Walk left (west) on High Street's rough asphalt. There are no sidewalks here, but little traffic interferes. The street is lined with small Victorian brick houses topped by detailed gables and eaves. The two-story Belford House with a distinctive flat roof and squared corners was built in 1876; it was the home of Judge James Belford, nicknamed the "Red-Headed Rooster of the Rockies." An early politician, attorney, and judge, Belford was Colorado's first elected Congressman. Note the mortarless stone walls near the street. The walls were laid by Cornish masons when cement was expensive and hard to get.

➤After a couple of blocks, High Street dead-ends on County Road. Turn left (south) on County and descend a short, narrow, and steep sidewalk to Eureka Street.

The large church on the left on the corner of Eureka and County is St. James Methodist Church. This is the oldest Protestant church in Colorado. The church was organized in 1859. Construction started on the hillside site in 1864, but lack of funds kept it from being finished until 1872. The church has ornate stained glass windows, eighty oak pews, and a large pipe organ.

of interest

Upper Eureka Street

If you want a longer walk than the one described, follow Eureka Street west up Eureka Gulch to find the town's five cemeteries at the head of the gulch. This adds 2 miles (1 mile up and 1 mile down) to the walk's length. The street passes numerous old residences of brick and frame construction. Many stone foundations and walls remain as a testament to earlier days.

Near the head of the gulch, on the left, is the ruin of Mack's Rocky Mountain Brewery, a large stone building. One of the largest breweries in Colorado Territory, Mack's was built in 1874 by Jake Mack. Besides beer, it offered a bowling lane and a beer garden.

At the top of the hill are Central City's five cemeteries. The largest is the Catholic Cemetery, slightly downhill and to the left. On the right, overgrown with wild grasses and small aspens, are the Protestant and Knights of Pythias cemeteries. A walk through these burying grounds reveals the trials and rigors of mining life, with graves of infants, mine casualties, women who died in childbirth, and victims of epidemics.■

➤Continue east on Eureka St. Down and across the street from the church is the Central City Opera House, one of the town's best known and most beloved landmarks. The native granite building is the state's oldest opera house. It opened on March 4, 1878, with a musical production by the local Amateur Dramatic Company. The building was designed by famed Denver architect Robert Roeschlaub and built by contractor Peter McFarlane. The acoustically perfect theater, seating 747 (tightly) in old wooden seats, is listed on the National Register of Historic Places.

Numerous stars appeared here, including actor Edwin Booth and Buffalo Bill Cody, playing to full houses.

The theater fell into disuse until it was revived in 1932 with a production of "Camille" starring film legend Lillian Gish. Now the Central City Opera House Association continues the long tradition of theater here by running three operas every summer featuring acclaimed singers.

The Opera Garden sits immediately east of the Opera House. This small garden and plaza, restored by a gift of May Bonfils-Stanton, features trees, a lawn, benches, and a U.S. Geological Survey benchmark that marks the elevation. The plaque reads, "You are now 8,464.296 feet above sea level—a perfect altitude for health and longevity."

➤Continue walking east from the Opera House on Eureka St. Adjacent to the opera house garden is the Teller House, another of Central City's most famous buildings. Now a casino, the hotel was built by Henry M. Teller in 1871 as the largest and most elegant hotel in Colorado Territory outside Denver. The five-story brick hotel cost $84,000 to build and offered 150 rooms. Numerous dignitaries stayed here, including President Grant. Today, the building's most popular attraction is the famous "Face on the Barroom Floor." *Denver Post* artist Herndon Davis painted the face of his wife Edna by candlelight one night in 1934. Protected by a sheet of glass, the face still peers up from the floorboards.

Across Eureka St. sits the small house that was Henry Teller's law office. Teller was also a prosperous attorney and one of Colorado's first two U.S. senators. The wood frame house, built in 1862, survived the disastrous town fires and was moved several times before coming to rest at its present location. Now it is the box office and gift shop for the Central City Opera House.

Next door to the law office is the old Williams Stables. This stablery was erected in 1876 for Teller House guests. The massive brick and stone building is dominated by imposing arches and old painted signs that offer "Carriages to Idaho Springs . . . and all Points of Interest."

➤At the corner of Eureka and Pine streets, turn right (south) and follow the east side of narrow Pine St. for a couple of blocks. You can see the back of Main Street's buildings below you, on the east side of the street, connected to your route by walkways and staircases.

One point of interest along Pine St. is the Rickville-Williams House on the left, just past the brick Henderson Block. This 1868 wood frame building, designed in Greek Revival style, escaped the town fires. Ironically, it was one of few Central City homes covered by fire insurance.

The obvious church on the right is St. Mary's of the Assumption Catholic Church. Central City's first Catholic mass was held in 1860. In 1869 Bishop John Lamy from Santa Fe laid the cornerstone for this church, which was completed in 1892. Dominated by its towering steeple, the brick church exemplifies the Gothic Revival style.

Just past the church is the lovely Parish-Penrose House. Built after the 1874 fire, it served as the church rectory until the 1940s.

➤Continue down Pine St., angling left onto Bourion Street where Pine climbs steeply to the right. This uphill section of Pine was long known as "The Hill," Central City's red-light district. Two brothels were located in the fancy houses up the street.

➤Keep going left down Bourion St. past a small brick cottage and a brick house. Both have exquisite decorative brickwork similar to houses on Pine St.

➤At the intersection of Bourion and Nevada streets, turn left (northeast) and walk along the sidewalk back to City Hall and the start of the walk. Check out the detailed, painted mural that is a composite of Central City's history, including the railroad, mining, the great fires, and the town's distinctive buildings.

Walk **18**

Castlewood Canyon State Park

General location: Along the rocky canyons in Cherry Creek in Castlewood Canyon State Park, southeast of Denver.

Special attractions: Scenic views, nature study, wildlife, and rock climbing.

Difficulty rating: Two walks, one easy and one difficult.

Distance: The Canyon View Nature Trail is 0.7 mile. The Inner Canyon–Lake Gulch Loop is 2 miles.

Estimated time: 1 to 3 hours.

Services: No services on the trails. Drinking water, restrooms, books, and information are available at the visitor center. Franktown, to the immediate north, is the nearest town with services.

Restrictions: You'll need a daily pass or annual permit to visit the park. Stay on designated trails. Mountain bikes are only allowed on park roads. Pets must be on a leash. Ground fires are prohibited. Gathering of artifacts, vegetation, and timber is prohibited. Some winters, snow prohibits travel on the Inner Canyon Trail.

For more information: Castlewood Canyon State Park.

Getting started: Drive south from Denver on Interstate 25 to Exit 182 at Castle Rock. Head east for 6 miles on Colorado Highway 86 to Franktown. Turn south at the crossroads onto Colorado Highway 83 and drive 5 miles to the marked park turnoff. Turn right (west) and drive along the rim 0.5 mile to the visitor center. The Canyon View Nature Trail walk begins at the Bridge Canyon Overlook parking area, just past the visitor center on the right. To reach the Inner Canyon–Lake Gulch Loop Trail, drive northwest from the visitor center to the large parking area at the road's end called Canyon Point. The trail begins on the north side of the lot.

Public transportation: None.

Overview: Cherry Creek springs from the rolling hills of Palmer Divide, a forested ridge that separates the Platte and Arkansas River watersheds between Denver and Colorado Springs. The creek twists northward through grasslands and cattle ranches for 15 miles before slicing into the coarse rock layers at Castlewood Canyon. Much of the 10-mile canyon southeast of Denver is protected in 873-acre Castlewood Canyon State Park.

With 19 inches of rainfall annually, the park harbors groves of ponderosa pine and Douglas-fir on north-facing slopes. Quaking aspens, growing far below their normal 8,000- to 10,000-foot range, flourish in moist canyon draws. Grassy meadows splotched with summer wildflowers border the inner canyon, while twisted juniper and dense copses

Castlewood Canyon

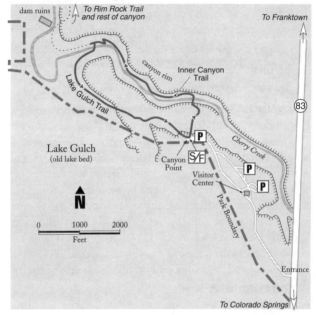

of scrub oak grow along the stony rim. Numerous hiking trails and walking paths lace this secret getaway. Castlewood Canyon's dense woodlands, tumbling water, and rough-hewn cliffs offer walkers an opportunity to discover and explore ecological diversity and unique scenery. Visitors here can picnic under the pines and observe wildlife.

This entry describes two of Castlewood's best walks. The Inner Canyon–Lake Gulch Loop Trail is a moderately rough trail that explores the canyon north of the park's visitor center. The Canyon View Nature Trail is a paved, wheelchair-accessible path along the west rim of the canyon. Stay on the trails to avoid problems. Loose rock often comes off the

East Facilities-Castlewood Canyon

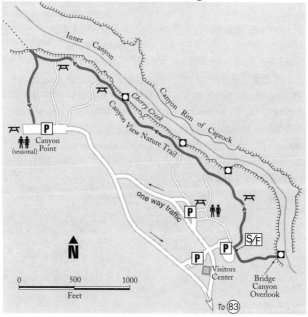

cliffs; leave rock climbing to experienced climbers with proper equipment. Beehives and wasps' nests are found in cavities and cracks on the cliffs. Mosquitoes can be a problem in summer; carry bug spray to ward them off.

The walk

►Begin at the large parking area near the picnic pavilions. Restrooms and drinking fountains (closed in winter) are located here. Find the small sign for the Inner Canyon Trail on the north side of the lot. Also, look for the large sign for

185

the Canyon View Nature Trail with a map of the lower canyon.

➤Walk north on the paved trail, dropping slightly toward the canyon rim. Scattered ponderosa pines and junipers dot the rim, as do groves of scrub oak and open meadows. Picnic tables also sit near the rim.

➤At the canyon rim, the paved path intersects the marked Inner Canyon Trailhead. Follow this trail straight ahead.

➤The narrow, gravel Inner Canyon Trail drops steeply downhill, winding through cliff bands and tall scrub oaks. Watch your footing on the steep sections, particularly if ice or snow are present.

➤The trail emerges onto the boulder-strewn floor of Castlewood Canyon and crosses gurgling Cherry Creek on a wooden plank bridge to the creek's north bank. Head northwest above the creek for about 0.75 mile, passing many large, lichen-covered boulders and plunging through a dense scrub oak forest. The moist slopes on the opposite side of the canyon are thick with tall spruces, Douglas-firs, and ponderosa pines.

Stop along the way and look at one of the immense boulders beside the trail, which tumbled from the cliff rim above. The 25-million-year-old rock here is known as Castle Rock Conglomerate. The geological formation stretches along the east and west canyon rims. The concrete-hard rock, deposited in an ancient river, is coarsely studded with volcanic pebbles and cobbles that jut out at odd angles.

The trail heads northwest and the canyon slowly deepens.

➤At the mouth of the Inner Canyon, the trail intersects Lake Gulch Trail. This 0.9-mile trail heads south-southeast back to the walk's start. The Inner Canyon Trail continues 0.2 mile northwest to the old dam ruins where it joins

Walker crossing Cherry Creek, Castlewood Canyon.
MARTHA MORRIS PHOTO

the Creek Bottom and Rim Rock trails. Pick up a park map at the visitor center for information on these trails.

➤Take a left on the Lake Gulch Trail. You'll drop down to the creek and cross it via a wooden plank bridge. Edge up the trail on the bank above the creek to a gravel bench.

➤Follow the trail along the bench, trending left around a forested headland, to reach the western side of the hill.

of interest

Canyon View Nature Trail

Visitors in wheelchairs or those with small children and strollers will enjoy the Canyon View Nature Trail, a paved 0.7-mile trail that traverses the west rim of Castlewood Canyon. This walk offers marvelous views into the canyon from a series of rim-edge viewpoints. The walk can be started from either the parking lot for the Bridge Canyon Overlook, just east of the visitor center, or at the large parking area at the end of the park road where the Inner Canyon Trail begins. This description begins from the parking area near the visitor center.

First, go 400 feet down a paved trail to Bridge Canyon Overlook. This viewpoint, which is not wheelchair-accessible, offers a great view into the canyon below and a look at a nearby highway bridge. Retrace your steps back to the parking area and follow the marked trail northwest along the canyon rim past three more viewpoints to the start of the Inner Canyon Trail. From here you can head south up a slight hill to the parking area and restrooms at the northwest terminus of the park road, then follow a roadside bike path back to your car. Or, even better, retrace your steps back to the parking lot by following the nature trail. The scenery looks better the second time through, anyway!■

►The trail gradually ascends, passing scrub oak copses and scattered pines. To the west, a broad grassy valley is dotted with grazing cattle and a couple of ranch houses and barns. Beyond the valley's western rim rises the snowcapped Front Range.

This valley was once part of a large lake formed by a dam, downstream to the northwest where the canyon constricts. The earthen dam, built in 1890, was used for flood control, irrigation, and recreation. The year after it was built, a panel of state engineers examined leakage and determined that the dam had been built by "irresponsible contractors under inadequate supervision." The dam's foundation was slowly weakened by a natural spring until the night of August 3, 1933, when a heavy rainstorm burst the dam and sent a 30-foot cascade of water surging toward Denver. The flood caused two deaths, more than $1 million in damage, and excavated a deep channel through Castlewood's lower canyon. The ruins of the dam still straddle the canyon narrows below the Inner Canyon Trail.

►Atop the rimrock, the trail enters a ponderosa pine forest. Stop and sniff the trees' rough bark. The pine has a distinctive smell similar to butterscotch or vanilla. Note where the bark has been gnawed or girdled by porcupines in search of the sweet inner cambium during cold winters, when other food is buried by snow.

►Follow the trail southeast along flat ground to the picnic pavilions, parking area, and the walk's end.

Walk 19
Roxborough State Park

General location: The Fountain Valley, in Roxborough State Park southwest of Denver at the base of the mountains.

Special attractions: Spectacular sandstone formations, scenic views, wildlife, visitor center displays, and interpretative programs.

Difficulty rating: Difficult. There are some gentle uphill and downhill sections on the gravel path.

Distance: 2.2 miles.

Estimated time: 2 hours.

Services: Restrooms and drinking water at the park visitor center.

Restrictions: You must pay a daily use fee to enter the park. Pay at the self-serve entrance station or at the visitor center.

Stay on designated trails. Do not climb any rock formations. Pets are not allowed in the park. No fires or firearms allowed. Pack out all litter, including cigarette butts. Collecting rocks, wood, or plants is prohibited. Most trails are closed to horses and mountain bikes. Day use only; park gates are locked at night.

For more information: Roxborough State Park.

Getting started: Reach the park by driving southwest from Denver on Santa Fe Drive, which turns into U.S. Highway 85. Continue south out of town to Titan Road. Turn right (west) and follow Titan Rd., which eventually bends south and turns into North Rampart Range Road. About 6.6 miles from US 85, turn left on Roxborough Park Road. Follow the dirt road for 2.1 miles through the park's entrance station to the visitor center

Public transportation: None.

Overview: Stunning Roxborough State Park is one of the crown jewels of Colorado's state park system. The 3,245-acre parkland, nestled against the Front Range southwest of Denver, is a refuge filled with nature in the raw. The marvelous scenery here is dominated by a natural rock architecture of soaring sandstone slabs, pinnacles, hogbacks, and buttresses. Its shallow, cliff-walled valleys teem with diverse plants and wildlife.

A meeting place for plants and animals from both the mountains and the prairie, Roxborough boasts nine distinct plant communities within its fertile valleys and on its dry slopes. Dense thickets of Gambel oak or scrub oak crowd the hillsides. Lush meadows spread a carpet of grasses and wildflowers in spring and summer. Ponderosa pine and Douglas-fir thrive on moister slopes, while quaking aspen, rare

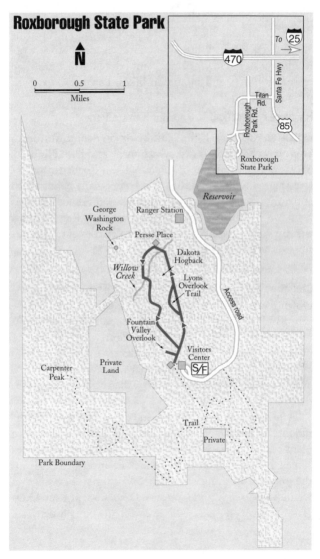

Roxborough State Park

N

0   0.5   1
Miles

To I-25

470

Santa Fe Hwy

Titan Rd.

Roxborough Park Rd.

85

Roxborough State Park

Reservoir

Ranger Station

George Washington Rock

Persse Place

Willow Creek

Dakota Hogback

Lyons Overlook Trail

Access road

Fountain Valley Overlook

Visitors Center

S/F

Carpenter Peak

Private Land

Trail

Private

Park Boundary

at a 6,000-foot elevation, tuck against the towering sandstone cliffs. Many animals call the park's varied habitats home, including coyote, red fox, porcupine, raccoon, weasel, bobcat, and mule deer. An elk herd ranges into the park from the adjoining peaks to the west, along with the occasional mountain lion and foraging black bear. Golden eagles, red-tailed hawks, magpies, and towhees are among the 112 bird species that have been seen here. Common snakes are the prairie rattlesnake, bullsnake, and yellow-bellied racer.

A designated Colorado Natural Area, National Archeological District, and National Natural Landmark, the park preserves and protects this special undeveloped slice of Colorado's Front Range ecology. Roxborough is an enclave of wilderness treasures and natural diversity, offering visitors a superlative glimpse into the state's rich natural heritage. This is not a place to come to for recreation; instead, it's a tranquil place for hiking and nature study. To preserve the delicate rock formations and brushy valleys, rock climbing, off-trail hiking, mountain biking, cooking, and campfires are prohibited.

Walkers will find a variety of trails here, including the excellent 2.2-mile Fountain Valley Trail, the 1.5-mile Willow Creek Loop Trail, and the 6-mile Carpenter Peak Trail. The Fountain Valley Trail, described here, is perhaps the best of the park's trails. The wide gravel path winds through scenic Fountain Valley, climbs to a lofty overlook, passes through dense oak woodlands, and crosses wide meadows studded with wildflowers. The loop is accessible to walkers with kiddie strollers, offering moderate grades and elevation gains. Plenty of shaded benches allow you to enjoy views and conversations, and a self-guided natural history trail guide corresponds to numbered posts along the path. (Buy or borrow a trail guide at the visitor center.) Stay on the trail to avoid resource damage; keep a sharp eye out for rattle-snakes. Poison ivy is common in the scrub oak forest along-side the trail. Carry water, especially on warm days.

The walk

➤The 2.2-mile Fountain Valley Trail begins at the Roxborough State Park Visitor Center just north of the park-ing lots. Reach the center by walking up a short paved path that begins on the right side of the upper lot, or by follow-ing the service road to the left.

The visitor center offers interpretive displays that detail Roxborough's geology and natural history. It also houses a small bookstore and gift shop. Park naturalists can answer almost any use question. A variety of naturalist-guided activities are available to visitors, particularly on weekends. These include full-moon hikes, drawing workshops, geol-ogy hikes, slide programs, and children's storytime. Ask about the monthly schedule.

➤Exit the main doors of the visitor center and walk west a few steps past the patio to the beginning of the trail. Turn right and walk north past the first interpretive stop with an aerial photograph of the trail and the park.

➤Head north on the wide gravel path, up a gentle grade below airy ridges of Fountain Formation sandstone. Dense copses of Gambel oak line the trail. Look for the three-lobed shiny leaflets of poison ivy in the oak shade. The ivy turns brilliant red and yellow in autumn. This poisonous plant causes an itchy rash on the skin of anyone unfortunate enough to touch it. For your sake and theirs, don't let chil-dren clamber through the ivy. Hemlock is another poisonous plant common here. Growing on a tall, woody stem that can reach 5 feet or more, hemlock has small leaves that

of interest

Roxborough's Early Residents

The area that is now Roxborough State Park was popular with Native Americans. Its earliest inhabitants were Paleo-Indians who butchered mammoths, horses, and camels at Lamb Spring. This site, with pre-Clovis period stone artifacts as many as twelve thousand years old, lies between Roxborough State Park and Chatfield Reservoir. These early people had a big-game hunting tradition, depending on large mammals for food, hides for clothing and shelter, bones for tools, and sinew for sewing.

The park itself boasts significant archaeological treasures. One survey uncovered forty-four prehistoric sites, primarily campsites, quarry stations, and work areas, with evidence of seasonal human occupation over the last five thousand years. Roxborough State Park is a designated National Archaeological District.

In historic times, the Apache Indians ranged through here until the 1700s, when the Comanches, a Plains tribe, and the Utes, a mountain tribe, displaced them. The Cheyenne and Arapaho Indians came onto Colorado's high plains in the late 1700s and occasionally skirmished with Ute hunters along the Front Range.■

resemble parsley. Used by Indians to poison arrow tips, hemlock was the ancient Greek philosopher Socrates' poison of choice for his suicide.

►After about 0.25 mile, look for the Fountain Valley Overlook side trail on your left. This short uphill walk yields a spectacular view north into Fountain Valley and over its tilted sandstone slabs. Looking farther north you can see long-stretching hogbacks, Green Mountain, and the Front Range escarpment. A bench lets you rest and meditate on the view.

➤Returning to the main trail, continue north. The path gently descends and bends into a broad meadow. Keep right at the obvious Y-junction.

This spot, Stop 4 in the trail guide, offers a good look at the park's major rock formations. The prominent hogback to the right (east) is the Dakota hogback, a serrated spine of uplifted Dakota sandstone deposited some 100 million years ago during the Cretaceous Period as beach and floodplain sediments were left along an encroaching coastline. Footprints of dinosaurs are often found on the Dakota's rippled sandstone, deposited on those long-ago beaches.

The middle hogback is composed of Lyons Formation sandstone, a much older rock that was deposited as sand dunes in an ancient desert. On the left (west) is the Fountain Formation, a thick layer of ruddy sandstone that was horizontally deposited as alluvial runoff during the Pennsylvanian Period between 325 and 280 million years ago. Evidence of stream deposition is readily apparent if you look carefully at the rock matrix. Notice the rough assortment of rocks, ranging from rounded cobbles to smooth river pebbles to coarse gravel and sand.

To the far left, the Front Range holds the area's oldest rocks, billion-year-old igneous rocks formed deep within the earth's crust and metamorphic rocks that were altered by intense heat and pressure. The rock layers were later uplifted and tilted during the Laramide mountain building period, about 70 million years ago. Water sculpted and stripped away the softer layers and left behind the resistant hogbacks seen today. When you gaze at this monumental sculpture garden, remember that Roxborough's geologic layers are like an immense book, with each rock strata representing a chapter in the greater story. Each formation tells its own tale of strange worlds, the raising and eroding of great mountains, and the passage of various lifeforms.

➤Angle northeast on the path across a broad, grassy swale that dips and funnels eastward to a sharp gap in the Dakota hogback. Thick groves of scrub oak and mountain mahogany, a favorite deer food, line the left side of the path. The meadows here comprise tall grasses, wildflowers, and occasional yuccas with sharp, spiked leaves. More than fifty grass species are found in the park. Common animal inhabitants of the grasslands include pocket gophers (which leave mounds of soil near their underground burrows), coyotes, rattlesnakes, and bullsnakes.

➤As the trail ascends north toward a low pass, look for the Lyons Overlook Trail on the left. The Lyons Trail steps up several railroad ties before climbing through a narrow swath cut through the scrub oak. This short side-trail climbs northwest and west to the crest of the Lyons hogback and a fenced wooden platform that lets you peer west into the heart of Fountain Valley. The valley below is hemmed in by lofty sandstone slabs with hues of brick red, salmon pink, orange, and maroon. The red tint comes from the oxidation of iron in the rock. The smooth sheets of sandstone, tilted upward at a 60-degree angle, are grooved and broken into sharp buttresses and airy ridges. Good views along the hogbacks reach north toward the Front Range peaks. Twisted ponderosa pines grow along the crest near the viewpoint, finding moisture and minerals in the dry, sandy soils. The ponderosa pine, a common Colorado conifer, yields a distinctive butterscotch or vanilla smell to those who sniff its bark.

➤Follow the overlook trail downhill and regain the main path on a gentle downhill. Go left. The slowly descending trail follows a broad grassy ravine northward. The gully along the trail is the eroded remnant of an old road that paralleled today's route. Heavy thunderstorms carved out the gully along the old wagon ruts.

At the bottom of the draw is the old Persse Place. Here sit a couple of sagging log cabins with tin roofs, as well as a cedar-roofed stone house shingled with a spacious north-facing porch. Henry S. Persse was a Denver entrepreneur who acquired much of the land in today's Roxborough State Park. Although the area was first named Washington Park for a fanciful profile of George Washington in the rocks to the west, Persse renamed the area Roxborough Park after his Irish family estate. After 1902, Persse used the area as a summer home and planned to turn it into a luxurious resort for Denver's well-heeled elite. His dream was never realized, but the park was a popular place in the early twentieth century. Denver's famous mayor Robert Speer wrote in 1910 that the park "should be owned by the city for the free use of the people." It took many decades before the state purchased the first 500 acres for the park in 1975. Subsequent purchases of available land have expanded the park to its current size. Roxborough officially opened to public use in 1987.

The stone house at the Persse Place was built in 1903 from local Lyons sandstone. The dilapidated log buildings to the south may have been erected as early as the 1870s by Denis Cooper; they were used by Persse as a blacksmith/tool shed and a chicken coop. The Persse family maintained a residence in Denver, using the house here as a seasonal retreat. John Persse, Henry's son, lived here from 1907 until 1937. Horace Persse, Henry's youngest son, stayed in a brick house on Sundance Ranch, on the park's south side. Henry Persse was killed in 1918 after being hit by a streetcar on Colfax Avenue in Denver. The Persse Place is listed on the National Register of Historic Places.

►The trail bends west at the cabins, crosses trickling Little Willow Creek, and enters Fountain Valley proper. Dense vegetation lines the moist creek banks, including tall

Sandstone formations, Roxborough State Park.

cottonwoods, willows, Rocky Mountain maples, and chokecherry thickets. Riparian corridors such as this one are rich habitats for birds and animals.

➤After entering the valley, trend southward alongside a broad meadow that is blanketed with wildflowers in late spring and summer. At Post 12, look west across the meadow to the looming sandstone slab known as George Washington Rock. With an imaginative eye, you can detect the sky-turned profile of our first president with his beaklike nose and sloped forehead. This profile gave the valley the name Washington Park until the early 1900s.

➤The trail edges south between the lush creekbed and a wide, reseeded meadow. West of Post 15 is a flat, marshy plain filled with sedges and scouring rushes or horsetails. The marsh is often flooded by a shallow pond after a wet spring, creating an ideal habitat for frogs, ducks, and great blue herons. Willows line the marshy area.

Willow Creek Loop Trail

Another good Roxborough State Park walk follows the easy 1.5-mile Willow Creek Loop Trail. This narrow path offers gentle grades through various habitats including scrub oak woodland, open meadows, and a creekside riparian area. A park brochure leads walkers along the trail, with fifteen interpretive stops. The trail guide brochure is available for purchase or loan at the visitor center. Allow up to 1 hour to walk the trail.

The trail begins just west of the visitor center. Look for a sign that points the way to Carpenter Peak, the park's high point. The path heads south through dense scrub oak below sandstone slabs. Keep left at the obvious trail junction; the right fork leads up the South Rim and Carpenter Peak trails. From here the path crosses an old ranch meadow and descends to Willow Creek. Lush vegetation, including a towering ponderosa pine, lines the creek. The walk heads east to another trail junction. Keep left and descend north to a wooden bridge over the creek. The park road and parking area are north of the bridge. Follow a short trail along the road to the upper parking lot and the visitor center. ■

➤The walk slowly ascends in the valley, twisting below castellated sandstone spires and flat rock slabs. You'll find shade amid thick groves of scrub oak. Aspens and Douglas-fir nestle on the moist hillsides below the slabs west of Post 17. Both are relatively rare at this low elevation. Botanists speculate that the aspens may be a relic stand left over from the last ice age, when the climate was cooler and wetter than it is today. The aspen leaves bring a brilliant gold color to warm October days, offering a counterpoint to the red rocks.

You will get good views of the sandstone slabs that hem in the valley's west edge from the trail as it swings across the wooded area. Rock amphitheaters echo with the raucous calls of jays and magpies. Other birds rustle in dried oak leaves. A cascade of scrub oak spills down steep gullies cut into the slabs.

➤As the walk ascends and heads south, the valley slowly widens. Several benches, under shady trees, allow you to take a break and meditate on Roxborough's spectacular scenery and natural diversity. Eventually, the trail reaches the Y-junction and rejoins the first trail section. Continue south to the visitor center and the walk's end.

Appendix A: Other Sights, Other Walks

Colorado is a spectacular land of prairies, peaks, and plateaus. It is a place to discover and explore the beauty, diversity, and majesty of raw nature. It is also filled with historic Old West towns and landmarks, along with some of the world's best ski resorts. Its wilderness parks offer spectacular scenic views and superb outdoor recreational opportunities. Here are a few suggestions to help you further enjoy Colorado on foot.

Metro Denver's Best Attractions

Black American West Museum

Buffalo Bill's Grave and Memorial Museum (Golden)

Colorado Railroad Museum

Colorado State Capitol

Coors Brewery (Golden)

Denver Art Museum

Denver Museum of Natural History

Denver Zoo

Elitch Gardens Amusement Park

Larimer Square

Molly Brown House

Red Rocks Amphitheater

U.S. Mint

Colorado Ski Country

The ski resorts scattered across Colorado's Rocky Mountains offer superior ski terrain and some of America's best snow, along with a wide variety of other outdoor activities. Within a day's drive of Denver is Summit County, with four major resorts; Vail; and City of Denver-owned Winter Park.

Summit County, accessed via Interstate 70 and the Eisenhower Tunnel through the Continental Divide, is home to Breckenridge, Keystone, Copper Mountain, Loveland, and Arapahoe Basin ski areas. The area's great skiing is complemented by factory outlet stores, excellent restaurants, and lots of hiking trails that thread through the woodlands and up the lofty peaks. Vail, farther west on I-70, is North America's largest ski mountain and most popular ski resort.

Rocky Mountain National Park

Straddling the Continental Divide northwest of Denver, Rocky Mountain National Park protects a swath of pristine high country. The 415-square-mile park features 113 peaks above 10,000 feet, with 14,255-foot Longs Peak as its high point. It also boasts more than 150 lakes and 500 miles of rivers and streams. One-third of the park lies above timberline in the frigid alpine zone, where summer makes only a brief stop each year.

The park is filled with things to do and places to go. Trail Ridge Road, one of America's most inspired drives, winds 45 miles along the divide, offering inspired views of the aptly named Never Summer Range. Numerous hiking trails course through valleys and mountains. Herds of elk, deer, and bighorn sheep roam the park. The park offers five campgrounds. For more information, see FalconGuides *Scenic Driving Colorado* by Stewart M. Green and *Hiking Colorado* by Caryn and Peter Boddie.

Pikes Peak Country

Pikes Peak looms over Colorado Springs, 70 miles south of Denver. This 14,110-foot landmark dominates the Front Range like no other mountain, lifting its snowcapped ridges into the azure sky. Colorado Springs sprawls across the prairie east of the great peak. The city has superb mountain views, wide tree-lined streets, many historic sites, and loads of outdoor recreation opportunities. The Garden of the Gods is a city park filled with spectacular soaring sandstone formations. The U.S. Air Force Academy is the state's most popular tourist attraction, 10 miles north of downtown Colorado Springs. Make sure you tour the museum, visit the seventeen-spire Cadet Chapel, and watch the cadets march at lunchtime. On the south side of town, the Broadmoor Hotel is a renowned five-star resort with three golf courses. Other area attractions include the U.S. Olympic Training Center, the Pro Rodeo Hall of Fame, the Pikes Peak Highway, and, farther afield, the Cripple Creek–Victor National Historic District and the Royal Gorge. For more information, see *Walking Colorado Springs* by Judith Galas and Cindy West, a FalconGuide.

Appendix B: Contact Information

Most area attractions, museums, shops, restaurants, and visitor centers have schedules and informative materials. Contact them to confirm locations, hours, and entrance fees of sites mentioned in the walk descriptions. Below is a partial list of phone numbers and addresses of places mentioned in this guide. Places and contacts are listed in alphabetical order rather than by region or city.

Visitor Information

Boulder Chamber of Commerce
2440 Pearl Street
Boulder, CO 80302
(303) 442-1044

City of Central City
P.O. Box 278
Central City, CO 80427
(800) 542-2999

Colorado Springs Convention and Visitors Bureau
104 South Cascade Avenue
Colorado Springs, CO 80903
(719) 635-7506 or (800) DO-VISIT

Denver Metro Convention and Visitors Bureau
225 West Colfax Avenue
Denver, CO 80202
(303) 892-1112

Regional Transportation District (RTD)
1600 Blake Street
Denver, CO 80202
(303) 299-6000

Activities, Attractions, and Museums

Black American West Museum and Heritage Center
3091 California Street
Denver, CO 80205
(303) 292-2566

Colorado State Capitol
Broadway and Colfax
Denver, CO 80203
(303) 866-2604

Children's Museum of Denver
2121 Children's Museum Drive
Denver, CO 80211
(303) 433-7444

Colorado History Museum
13th Street and Broadway
Denver, CO 80203
(303) 866-3682

Colorado Railroad Museum
17155 West 44th Avenue
Golden, CO 80402
(303) 279-4591

Coors Brewing Company
13th and Ford Street
Golden, CO 80401
(303) 277-BEER

Denver Art Museum
14th and Bannock
Denver, CO 80204
(303) 640-4433

Denver Botanic Gardens
1005 York Street
Denver, CO 80206
(303) 331-4000

Denver Performing Arts Complex
14th and Curtis Street
Denver, CO 80204
(303) 893-4100

Denver Museum of Natural History
2001 Colorado Boulevard
Denver, CO 80205
(303) 322-7009

Denver Zoo
East 23rd Avenue
Denver, CO 80205
(303) 331-4110

Elitch Gardens Amusement Park
Denver, CO 80202
(303) 594-4FUN

Foothills Art Center
809 15th Street
Golden, CO 80401
(303) 279-3922

Forney Transportation Museum
1416 Platte Street
Denver, CO 80202
(303) 433-3643

Larimer Square
1400 Block of Larimer Street
Denver, CO 80202
(303) 534-2367

Lower Downtown District
1616 17th Street, #368
Denver, CO 80202
(303) 628-5428

Museum of Western Art
1727 Tremont Place
Denver, CO 80202
(303) 296-1880

Rocky Mountain Quilt Museum
1111 Washington Avenue
Golden, CO 80401
(303) 277-0377

United States Mint
West Colfax and Cherokee
Denver, CO 80202
(303) 844-3582

Parks

Adams County Parks Department
9755 Henderson Road
Brighton, CO 80601
(303)637-8000

Arvada Parks and Recreation Department
7800 West 62nd Avenue
Arvada, CO 80004
(303) 420-0984

Aurora Parks and Recreation Department
1470 South Havana, #502
Aurora, CO 80012
(303) 739-7168

Castlewood Canyon State Park
P.O. Box 504
Franktown, CO 80116
(303)688-5242

Denver Department of Parks and Recreation
2300 15th Street
Denver, CO 80202
(303) 964-2522

Denver Mountain Parks
2300 15th Street
Denver, CO 80202
(303) 964-2522

Englewood Parks
2800 South Platte River Drive
Englewood, CO 80110
(303) 786-2520

Foothills Park and Recreation District
2200 South Old Kipling
Lakewood, CO 80227
(303) 987-3602

Golden Parks and Recreation
1470 10th Street
Golden, CO 80401
(303) 384-8100

Lakewood Department of Parks and Recreation
445 South Allison Parkway
Lakewood, CO 80226
(303) 987-7800

Jefferson County Open Space
700 Jefferson County Parkway, Suite 100
Golden, CO 80401
(303) 271-5925

Rocky Mountain National Park
Estes Park, CO 80517
(970)586-1206

Roxborough State Park
4751 North Roxborough Drive
Littleton, CO 80125
(303)973-3959

Westminster Parks
4800 West 92nd Street
Westminster, CO 80030
(303) 430-2192

World Wide Web Sites

AOL—Digital City Denver
Keyword: Denver

Colorado Avalanche Home Page
http://www.nando.net/SportServer/hockey/nhl/que.html

Colorado Springs Convention and Visitors Bureau
http://www.coloradosprings-travel.com/CSCVB

Delightful in Denver
http://www.abwam.com/delightful

Denver Broncos
http://nflhome.com/teams/broncos/broncos.html

Denver Graphic City Guide
http://www.futurecast.com/gcg/denver.html

Denver International Airport (DIA)
http://infodenver.denver.co.us/~aviation/index.html

The *Denver Post* Newspaper
http://www.denverpost.com/

Denver Public Library
http://www.denver.lib.co.us/

The Downtown Denver Guide
http://www.downtown-denver.com

Hot Wired: Rough Guide to Denver
http://www.hotwired.com/rough/usa/rockies/co/

InfoDenver (City and County of Denver)
http://infodenver.denver.co.us

Inside Denver—*Rocky Mountain News*
http://InsideDenver.com/

Regional Transportation District—RTD (Bus service and schedules)
http://www.rtd-denver.com

The Weather Channel (latest weather)
http://www.weather.com/weather/us/cities/CO_Denver.html

Westword (weekly newspaper and events calendar)
http://www.westword.com

Appendix C: Great Tastes

The Denver area offers more than two thousand restaurants for your culinary delight. Epicures will discover a world of varying taste sensations, including classic Tex-Mex fare, several Oriental cuisines, elegant Continental-style bistros, coffee shops, and Old West camp cookery. Denver has been dubbed the "Napa Valley of Beer" for its numerous breweries. The city brews more beer than any other American city. Downtown Denver offers fifteen brew pubs and microbreweries alone.

The region's gastronomic variety makes it impossible to detail, describe, and recommend all the different restaurants in the small space here. It's best to explore Denver's eateries on your own, making your own restaurant choices and discoveries.

The Denver Metro Convention and Visitors Bureau offers a comprehensive listing of restaurants in its annual *Official Visitors Guide*. The cuisine categories are American, Asian, BBQ, Breakfast, Brew Pubs, Buffets, Chinese, Coloradoan, Continental, Cuisine Courante, Delis, French, German, Indian, Italian, Japanese, Korean, Mexican, Middle Eastern, Pizza, Southwestern, Steakhouses, Thai, and Vietnamese. Bon appetit!

Appendix D: Useful Phone Numbers

Denver Police
Emergency 911
Non-emergency (303) 640-2011

Fire and Rescue Services
Emergency 911
Non-emergency (303) 640-3435
Poison Control (303) 629-1123

Hospitals
Children's Hospital (303) 861-8888
Denver General Hospital (303) 436-6000
St. Joseph Hospital (303) 837-7111
Presbyterian/St. Luke's Medical Center (303) 839-6000

Libraries
Denver Public Library (303) 640-8800
Jefferson County Libraries:
Littleton (303) 932-2690
Arvada (303) 456-0780
Golden (303) 279-4585
Boulder Public Library (303)441-3100

Newspapers
The Denver Post (303) 820-1010
The Rocky Mountain News (303) 892-5000

Road Conditions
Statewide (303) 639-1111 or (303) 639-1234

Transportation
American Airlines (800) 433-7300
Amtrak (800) 872-7245
Continental Airlines (303) 398-3000
Delta Airlines (303) 696-1322

Denver International Airport (303) 342-2200
Frontier Airlines (303) 371-7000
Northwest Airlines (800) 225-2525
Regional Transportation District (RTD) (303) 299-6000
Trans World Airlines (800) 221-2000
Union Station (303) 534-2812
United Airlines (800) 241-6522

Weather Reports
Statewide (303) 398-3964

Appendix E: Read All About It

Want to learn more about Denver? The following books will get you started on its colorful history, points of interest, and recreational opportunities.

Boddie, Caryn, and Peter Boddie. *Hiking Colorado.* Helena, Mont.: Falcon Publishing, 1991.

> Follows the best hiking trails throughout Colorado.

Caurso, Laura, and Robert Ebisch. *The Insiders' Guide to Greater Denver.* Manteo, North Carolina: The Insiders' Guides/Landmark Publishing, 1994.

> A comprehensive guide for visitors to the greater Denver area.

D'Antonio, Bob. *Mountain Biking Denver–Boulder.* Helena, Mont.: Falcon Publishing, 1997.

> A guide to the best mountain bike rides in the northern Front Range.

Galas, Judith, and Cindy West. *Walking Colorado Springs.* Helena, Mont.: Falcon Publishing, 1997.

> A guide to eighteen great walking tours in nearby Colorado Springs.

Green, Stewart M. *Scenic Driving Colorado.* Helena, Mont.: Falcon Publishing, 1994.

> A superb guide to thirty of Colorado's best scenic drives.

Green, Stewart M., *Rock Climbing Colorado.* Helena, Mont.: Falcon Publishing, 1995.

> The only guide that covers all of Colorado's major climbing areas, including the best Denver climbing sites.

Leonard, Stephen J., and Thomas J. Noel. *Denver: Mining Camp to Metropolis.* Boulder: University Press of Colorado, 1990.

> A comprehensive account of Denver's history.

Index

Page numbers in *italics* are maps. Page numbers in **bold** are photos.

Meet the Author

MARTHA MORRIS PHOTO

Stewart M. Green is a freelance writer and photographer living in Colorado Springs. His photographs and writing regularly appear in many national publications, including *Climbing*, *Rock & Ice*, *Outside*, *Sierra*, and others. He specializes in rock climbing and adventure photography.

Stewart has been the author and photographer of many books for Falcon Publishing, including *Rock Climbing Colorado*, *Rock Climbing Utah*, *Scenic Driving New England*, *Scenic Driving Colorado*, and *Back Country Byways*. He is currently hard at work on other Falcon titles.

A WHOLE DIFFERENT KIND OF

Experience A Whole Different Kind of Wa

The American Volkssport Association, America's premie walking organization, provides noncompetitive sporting events for outdoor enthusiasts. More than 500 volksspor (translated "sport of the people") clubs sponsor walks in scenic and historic areas nationwide. Earn special award for your participation.

For a free general information packet,
including a listing of clubs in your state,
call 1-800-830-WALK. (1-800-830-9255)

American Volkssport Association is a nonprofit, tax-exempt, national organization dedicated to promoting the benefits of health and physical fitness for people of all ages.